3000 MILES PER HOUR IN EVERY DIRECTION AT ONCE

Books by Nick Mamatas

Kwangju Diary (translator, with Kap Su Seol)
Northern Gothic
Urban Bizarre (anthology)

3000 MILES PER HOUR IN EVERY DIRECTION AT ONCE:

ESSAYS AND STORIES

NICK MAMATAS

LIBRARY EMPYREAL
Helluo librorum

3000 MILES PER HOUR IN EVERY DIRECTION AT ONCE

Published in the United States by **Library Empyreal**
P.O. Box 36503, Canton, OH 44735
www.libraryempyreal.com

ISBN: 1-930997-31-0

CONTENTS

9. Introduction by Zoe Trope
13. The Daniel Boone Of Jersey City
22. Your Life, Fifteen Minutes From Now
27. Brother Theodore Is Dead
32. Time of Day
47. Do The Wall Street Hustle
50. The Armory Show
57. It's An Honor To Be Nominated
63. Impression Sunrise
71. Why I Flame
75. Joey Ramone Saves the World
89. The Dead Don't Stay Dead
92. Beer On Sunday
98. How to Rid the World of Good
108. The Birth Of Western Civilization
119. Old Boilers and Old Men
127. Scarlet Women Watch TV Till Dawn
138. Travel Between Heavenly Bodies

Dedication

To Mandy, who doesn't even like my work.
And for Alanna, who does.
And for Jody, who always wanted to have a book dedicated to her.

Acknowledgements

As usual, there are too many people to mention, but I'll do it anyway. First, Sean Wallace, for taking on this unmarketable project. Then there are the editors who published the stuff here in the first place: Frank J. Marcopolos, Craig Vasiloff, Mickey Z., Mary Anne Mohanraj, Tim "Timprov" Cooper, Missy and Keith Suicide, Patrick and Honna Swenson, Russ Kick, Brian Keene, Tom Beller, Laura Conaway, Jayson Whitehead, and Alex Burns. Uh, that's in no particular order, by the way.

The pages would be all over your lap if not for cover design wizard Shishalden Hanlen and cover photographer Liza Pavelich. Thanks to literary superstar Zoe Trope for taking time out of her busy marching band schedule to write something for me. And thanks to my agent Michele Rubin, for allowing me to commit this very special brand of career suicide, and all for you.

Dearest Nick,

Will you make out with me?

I know I'm seventeen and you're thirty-one and I live on the west coast and you're in Jersey and I'm gay and you're . . . um, yeah. But I'm a literary teen idol with a six-figure advance! You're a small press nobody! You should be licking my pink Chucks and obliging my every whim. Never forget that.

If I don't have another tongue in my mouth soon, I'm going to cry.

But let's not be distracted by my (sloppy) methods of seduction. I have a rather embarrassing question to ask, but I feel that in order to remain friends, we have to be honest with each other. While your new book is amazing, I had one problem with it. Well, five problems, actually. I wanted to touch myself a lot while reading your manuscript but I wasn't sure if I should. Have you ever noticed how difficult it is to get off to books when you actually know who wrote them? It's like the writer is standing right there, watching you with your hand in your crotch. What if, the next time we talked, you somehow knew what I'd done? And you asked me about it?

"So, Zoe, did you enjoy that piece about the aliens?"

"Um . . . which one?"

"The one you masturbated to, you pervert!"

"That really doesn't narrow things down at all . . . "

Now, before you refuse to ever shake my hand, let me defend myself.

Contrary to popular belief, I am not a jezebel, charlatan, or a lolita. I'm also not a prodigy, no matter what anyone says. Observe:

I think I was fifteen the first time I heard your name. Will Tupper was telling me about riding in your car and how he felt like he had been with a celebrity since you're so famous and everything. "What's his name?"

"Nick Mamatas," Will said. He always made it sound so easy! The syllables slid off his tongue and I could hear him, thousands of miles away, smirking with satisfaction. What an asshole. I mean, just because he could say your name and I couldn't. Not yet, at least. I hadn't really tried.

But then you came to my defense against a pig-headed reviewer, and I read your Livejournal and wrote you a letter and you helped me write papers for school and when I tried to tell Will about how much I'm in love with you, it was a mess. A disaster. A cacophony.

"Nick Mah-mat-moss, er, Mat-mo-ass, Mah-mah-mat-mose . . . Aw, shit." Prodigy my ass. The next time someone accuses me of being brilliant, I will quickly remind them I couldn't even say your last name and that I cheated on a quiz in 10th grade and my SAT scores were well under 1300. So there.

Anyway, Will was a very patient teacher. "Mama-toss. Just think of tossing your mom. Mama-toss."

"Mah-mah-toss . . . " I tried it on for size. "Mamatas! Mamatas! Hey, look at me! I can finally say his damn name!" I was exalted, beaming with pride. I felt like I'd joined some exclusive club. "Mamatas! Mamatas! Mamatas!"

Had Will been there, I think he would have slapped me. But instead, he just hung up the phone.

Maybe Will's just jealous because I love you more than him (shh, don't tell). But being young and adored is a rough job. I have to deal with critics, claims of fraud, taunts, and accusations of being bourgeois. I was photocopying a 'zine & my friend called me up just to tell me that it's okay to be bourgeois—some of his best friends are bourgeois, apparently. I don't know how using my aunt's copier for my 'zine or buying my own saddle stapler makes me bourgeois, but maybe it does. Or maybe he just liked saying bourgeois. It's a fun word. So, how do you deal with being called bourgeois? God, look who I'm asking.

I don't know why I'm telling you all this. With my luck, you'll publish it somewhere and permanently tarnish my image. And then Harper would disown me and my parents would take away all my pens and journals and I'd go crazy like the Marquis de Sade, except more sexually depraved.

But you're not that cruel.

Love times a hundred,
Zoe Trope

Zoe Trope is the author *Please Don't Kill the Freshman: A Memoir,* which will be released by HarperTempest in the fall. She can be contacted via e-mail at **zoe_trope@hotmail.com**.

The Daniel Boone of Jersey City

When I left the Lower East Side of Manhattan in 1996, the stores on either side of my building included a bodega that sold heroin out the back and an empty, bombed-out hole. Today, a "funky" bridal shop and a tattoo parlor stand in their places. When a tattoo parlor is a sign of urban renewal, you know the neighborhood was bad before. The rent for my apartment, a single room with a bathtub about a foot away from the oven, was $575 a month, and after the slashing of rent control protections and the boom of the downtown economy, is probably quite near $1000 today.

The invisible hand of the marketplace helped me across the river, to Jersey City. Several years later, the big boys of finance capital have caught wind of this smallish city on the wrong side of the river and, like Daniel Boone spotting chimney smoke on the horizon, it may be time for me to move on.

Jersey City isn't the Kentucky backwoods; it is the single most diverse city in America, even beating out New York City and Los Angeles in the number of ethnic, cultural and linguistic groups represented in force in the town. In the early 1990s, Jersey City and the surrounding area was home to the racist "dot buster" gangs of youths who attacked immigrants from the Indian sub-continent, but few traces of that antagonism remain. Blacks, Latinos, the remnants of the Polish, Italian and Irish ethnic communities have been joined by newcomers from Egypt, India, Pakistan and sub-Saharan Africa, and in the streets, peace reigns for the most part. In the boardrooms and ward offices though, a different set of relationships is brewing, relationships which may transform this city beyond all recognition and push the working class families and new immigrants out of yet another city. And I may be part of that plan.

THE RUST COMPANY OF NEW JERSEY in huge red neon greeted me when I moved to the Journal Square area at the beginning of last year. The sign is atop an office building and inexplicably dominates the local skyline.

"Why is it there?" asked my roommate Chris one day, of the sign, which has never managed to spell out the actual name of the company, The Trust Company of New Jersey, since we moved. "It can't really help for branding and marketing, can it?"

"Oh, well, it is strategically positioned. You see, back before the Hindenburg, this used to be part of the old Akron-to-New York dirigible route. Everyone coming into town would see the sign while sitting at little aluminum tables and drinking Singapore Slings. The trust company was King Shit back then."

"Wow, that really does make sense," he said.

"Yeah, well, I made it up," I said.

The sign is our only entertainment in this part of town. There are no little cafes, no funky bars, no clubs, no bookstores. The sign, also, thanks to poor upkeep, comments on the neighborhood like a Greek chorus with its occasional shuttering and its blinked-out letters. In this part of Jersey, only abandoned light bulbs tell the truth. I had been living in downtown Jersey City since 1997, eking out a living as a freelance writer. It was only a dollar to get to Manhattan, and the prices for everything were much lower in this town, which has been called the Left Bank, the West Borough, and even the "afterbirth" of New York City. For $700 a month, I got a basement apartment where I could stretch my arms without touching both walls. I paid my rent in cash to the landlord who lived upstairs. The city had already begun to revitalize the area: a former dumping ground for tires and rusted cars had been transformed into the Newport Mall, with an attendant hotel and huge Shop Rite. A high rise was built on another old dump. The area was an Enterprise Zone, so sales taxes were only 3%. Some friends of mine heard about the town and found cheap apartments as well. Brownstones could be had for under $400,000, so the inevitable happened. White people showed up. They had cars and some of them had little freedom flags ever-so-discreetly on the bumper. Not enough to make a political statement or even register as "out" but just enough to serve as a band-aid for social consciousness and perhaps pick up a date in the mall parking lot. My rent also went up to over $1000. I had to move. "Here comes the neighborhood," I told my landlord, and I headed west, deeper into the city.

I bought a house across town in the run-down Journal Square area. It was the center of the city once, but not much is there now except for the community college, a Jesuit college, a few cheap restaurants, a strip of 99 cent stores and a huge prescient sign with a burnt out **T**. If there really was a Rust Company of Jersey City, it would be doing a booming business on this side of town. Only fifteen minutes away from Manhattan, a two-family home can be had for less than $150,000. Downtown, young white people with punk outfits and cups of coffee would stop me on the street. "Thank God," they say, "you're white. You look cool. I'm so lonely here. Can we be friends?"

No. We can't.

Whiteness in downtown then, and in Journal Square now, is a mark, not the default. Some people think it means you are in their special little club. The We Don't Really Live In Jersey City, We Just Ended Up Here Club. Won't you join the club and do the things white folk do, like scurry past the Black kids on the corner, while wondering where the police are?

I won't. So I moved across town, where grocers renting Egyptian musicals outnumbered video stores, and where flyers promising to get-rich-quick schemes took the place of poetry reading announcements. I moved in Jersey's own rust belt, because I could afford to buy there, and my dark hair and skin allowed me to pass for Egyptian or Latino. I wasn't accosted by white people in the street for nearly a month.

Then someone fixed the **T** on the Trust Company sign. The **U** burnt out instead. **THE TRST COMPANY OF NEW JERSEY**, or "The Tryst Company of New Jersey." Jersey City is engaged in a tryst of sorts, with some of the top Wall Street firms. Goldman Sachs, PaineWebber, Salomon Smith Barney, Merrill Lynch, Deloitte & Touche, Morgan

Stanley Dean Witter, Lehman Bros., and most recently, Chase Manhattan Bank, have all moved or are planning to move some of their operations to Jersey City. Even in this booming economy, large capital is looking to cut costs, and as I found out four years before Chase Manhattan did, rent is cheap in Jersey City, at nearly half the price.

And for big business, the city is even cheaper than that.

Jersey City homeowners pay some of the highest property taxes in the country, but in order to attract finance capital, the city limits property taxes large businesses have to pay. Many residents—even the homeowners—are in the lowest income bracket (less than $36,000), and yet their total tax bill amounts to 15.6 percent of income compared to only 6.2 percent of those people in the top income bracket ($404,000 or more). In Jersey City, 34.2% of property is tax exempt, and much of it is on the "Gold Coast" of the city, where high rise residences, brokerage firms and banks squeeze in, and where 85% of over-the-counter stock trades in this country take place.

From the high rise condos near Exchange Place, a well-heeled resident may be able to catch a glimpse of a parking lot with a few rickety trailers. It isn't another high rise going up, it is an annex for a local public school, part of a system so bad and so underfunded that the state of New Jersey had to take it over in 1989. Republican Mayor Bret Schundler's remedies are typical of his ilk: vouchers and charter schools. Even with vouchers, the low-income families of Jersey City aren't often able to afford private school, and there simply aren't enough seats for all children who need them in the charter schools. The vouchers tend to go to the new residents, the high rise dwellers who can't imagine sending their kids to learn in a leaking tractor trailer, whether the trailer houses a public school or a charter school.

Property taxes, in essence, constitute a transfer payment from the working-class homeowners of the city to the big businesses on the Gold Coast. While nearly $1 billion has been invested in the Gold Coast region of Jersey City, much of the rest of the town is still suffering from high property taxes and poor schools. New Jersey spent $200 million more in 2001 to attract companies. Chase Manhattan is moving thanks to the corporate tax credits, the low rents, the employee training funds and the limited sales tax it will have to pay. Meanwhile, the city is offering no tax relief for most of its residents. The day I received my quarterly tax bill for over $1000 dollars (only three more to pay this year!), the **O** on the Trust Company sign expired bitterly. **THE TRST COMPANY F NEW JERSEY**. Fuck New Jersey.

In 1999, Mayor Schundler announced massive lay offs for city workers, citing budget shortfalls, in spite of crushing property taxes for most of the city's residents. The state of New Jersey was compelled by the judiciary to up the amount it spent on urban school districts, and in order to keep the state budget solvent, cut its aid to the rest of Jersey City, which found itself preparing to lay off 1,271 Jersey City employees, representing 58% of the City's total civilian workforce, 175 police officers, and 137 firefighters. The city blamed the state, then raised property taxes again. The subsidies for the Gold Coast continue unabated. F' New Jersey, indeed. Jersey City seems to be finding itself. In the Winter 2000 semester, I taught two courses for Hudson County Community College in Jersey City. The wage: $400 per credit, or 50% of what an adjunct instructor makes at a City University of New York community college ten minutes away.

The orientation: a listing of the buildings the college was going to buy. The training: one hour with a coordinator, to explain to me that attendance must be taken. Nobody mentioned that half of my students had never read a book. Concentrate on teaching them how to use Microsoft Word to type up papers, and how to use the World Wide Web to research instead of talking about rhetoric, I was told. Use the computer labs; major companies had provided some of the money for them. I couldn't even do that properly, thanks to Jersey City.

Instead of school-based email accounts (which are federally funded and have been available at most colleges since the mid-1980s), students were directed to make free hotmail accounts. The web-based hotmail isn't used in workplaces, except to surreptitiously shuttle porn past server firewalls. What are we training these students to do anyway? And of course, security guards closed the computer labs at 4PM, because nobody could possibly need a computer to type up a paper after 4PM. The vending machines and tv lounge remained open till 9PM.

One of my students was learning-disabled. I didn't find this out until five weeks into the course. A professional tutor for my English 101 class had "accidentally" gone to the wrong class section for the first seven weeks of the term. Six of my students had been in the United States for less than a year and pushed out of Basic English courses due to overcrowding. They simply had no chance to pass a college-level English course. And one student was legally blind. Unable to use a keyboard or monitor, barely able to write at age forty and still waiting for assistance from someone in the city, or someone in the school, to help her simply adjust her computer monitor so that it could display REALLY BIG LETTERS. None came, in direct violation of the Americans with Disabilities Act. She failed the course, too.

At one point late in the term, I asked the students to write about their favorite book. Nearly half my class had never read one. The college library literally contained fewer works of literature than my own home does. The city was doing about as much to fund learning in this college as it was doing to save its public schools: not much.

Unlike most colleges, where English 101 is sufficient, the HCCC 101 is considered so poorly designed that most four-year colleges won't even accept it as a transfer credit. Instead of repairing the 101 curriculum, the college simply made students take 102 as well, thus doubling the English and Humanities Division's income for basic writing courses. Additionally, students have to take the useless 'College Survival Skills' course, which does little more than remind them to go to class on time.

For students whose main problem with coming to class is taking care of their own children or attempting to hold onto their job while juggling school, the money spent on College Survival Skills could have been spent on pretty much anything else with better results. Daycare? Scholarships? Tuition reduction? Night courses? And then of course, there was attendance. I was never observed teaching (though the Assistant Dean made and broke two appointments to do so, violating college rules) but I damn sure had to take attendance every day, as if I was teaching high school or warehousing mental patients.

Examined as part of a greater Gold Coast strategy, the local community college and its poor funding and administration makes perfect sense. Jersey City, in order to defend its massive subsidies of wealthy corporations, needs to demonstrate that these companies provide jobs. My students, most of whom were computer science or accounting majors, and all of whom were convinced that they were going to "get a good job" and "be well-off" can work on Exchange Place. They weren't well-versed in literature, or even in developing simple English sentences, but most of them had basic computer skills and finally learned to show up on time.

They weren't going to be CPAs or software engineers, but an HCCC education prepared them to be the next generation of data entry clerks, security guards and janitors. The public will be satisfied when their kids start clinging to the bottom of the corporate ladder, and capital will have an array of faces of color for their brochures and corporate videos. The white kids of Jersey City, of course, skip HCCC and attend New Jersey City University (recently upgraded from a mere college with a new sign and some departmental juggling) or Saint Peter's College, a few blocks away from HCCC.

By concentrating urban renewal on a small sliver of the city, the rest of Jersey City becomes all the more desperate. Most of my students lived in homes owned by their families (often three or more generations were squeezed in) and they wanted out. If two more years in a poorly funded school promised a way out, who was I to tell them that they had better get used to the low wages and zero security of temp work? They could see the skyscrapers rising across town; if I was so smart, why was I in the slum with them, and not out there with the other white people? I quit after one semester, and raised the rents on the friends I was renting to to make up the lost income. So much for my f'ing principles. Then they fixed the **O**, but the **N** on the Trust Company sign burnt out.

THE TRUST COMPANY OF EW JERSEY.

Even with Chase Manhattan Bank moving into town, my Manhattan friends still stare at me when I mention my address in "Ew, Jersey!" Avenue B in Manhattan, where we used to loiter and litter with impunity while digging through garbage cans for soda bottles to return, has been redone into a strip of fancy stores. Alphabet City, once the home of squats and poor families, is now where my hipster friends took over. And they took over, thanks to jobs with bankrupt dot coms and family trust funds. They aren't pioneers like me, ready to explore bold new vistas of large apartments and inexpensive rents.

Since moving to Jersey City in 1997, I have lured fifteen other people across the river, most of them white and all of them college-educated. I was helping friends find nice places to live, I thought, but now I see that I too am simply part of the Gold Coast strategy. While I lived on handshake deals, the apartments I found for my friends were in apartment complexes. They talked to realtors, they found jobs with Paine Webber and Chase. After remaining stagnant for years, the ripples from my crossing the Hudson are beginning to spell higher rents. I bought to avoid paying $1400 for a three bedroom, two bathroom apartment (so what if it would have cost $5000 in Manhattan?). I raised the rents I collect now, to make up for tax increases. This will push my friends away from Journal Square and towards the Gold Coast, where they can walk (or be driven by corporate shuttles) to work and spend their money in swanky bistros and little boutiques. They can't handle the bodegas here, or the fact that the only supermarket is across town, next to the only major mall. They want air conditioning. They want doormen. And thanks to the money flowing into the Gold Coast, they can get it.

In the summer, I leave the front door to my building unlocked and ajar to let the draft in. We have never even heard of a crime occurring on this block. Yet one tenant reports being told to get off the porch by a cop who was worried about her. It isn't safe after sundown, he said, gangs will attack you right on your stoop. In the months we've been living here, we never saw any evidence of gang attacks or dangerous stoops, but the message was received.

Chris, who works for Chase Manhattan Bank, left for Manhattan one evening, but then came back home two minutes later. He couldn't cross the street to get to the PATH train, because there were "a whole mob of homeboys on the corner." They weren't violent, or threatening towards him, and there were only two of them, "but still . . . " he said, as if I could finish the sentence myself. A week later he admitted that it was just too sultry to walk the seven blocks to the train, and he didn't feel like hanging out with his friends in the Upper West Side that night anyway. The homies were just a convenient excuse. He joined the White Guy's club. It never occurred to him that since it was ninety-five degrees and since most of the apartments on the corner don't have air conditioning, that people may stay outside to socialize and cool off. Or maybe he did know this, "but still . . . "

Then there is the upstairs tenant, who keeps a pistol-grip shotgun (a gift from his grandfather, a former steel-mill Pinkerton who was issued the gun to blow away union men in the case of a sit-down strike) under his bed, in case of "home invasion." He is a law student at New York University, and told the neighbors that he was going to fight "for the people" after graduation, to make sure he was liked and admired on the block. He's going into corporate law next year. And these are the most progressive of my friends, the ones with working class backgrounds and a distrust of the system. I cleared the path with them, and on the horizon, we can see corporate chimneys rising, with the threat of gentrification looming. They're ready to turn back, and take their rightful places as conquering heroes in the upper middle class. Me, I'm looking West. I hear that there are abandoned paint factories in Harrison, and that the rents there are very cheap. *Ew, Jersey,* I can hear them all say, but they'll follow me eventually, and I'll have played my part in the destruction of another working class neighborhood.

January, 2001

Your Life, Fifteen Minutes From Now

It was 9:15 AM when they came for me, their breath stinking of champagne and cocktail franks. It must have been something I said the night before, or the way I looked on television when Mission Control lost contact with my brother. It was my turn though, and I had until 9:30 to make it last. I had a tuxedo on under my jumpsuit, and slipped out of it as the paparazzi flooded the street with the white light of their camera flashes. Blinded, I felt the hands of the people grabbing at my sleeves, my hands, my hair. The countdown had begun.

The party was in the streets, the way it always was, but this time, the people turned to me and cheered. "Where did you work before?" some flashbulb asked as it blinded me. "The factory, like the others. I worked in the factory. I made pigs in blankets." My answer didn't matter. A microphone asked me about my brother, but the eggbeater whipping of helicopter rotors coming in low to take my picture drowned out my answer. My brother was dying in space, and he hadn't even spent his fifteen minutes of fame yet. It was my turn. I looked up to the sky but only saw advertisements drawn across the night clouds with laser light. Beyond the logos and thirty-story-tall holographic breasts were stars I couldn't see. I didn't even see the hands pulling me into the crowded streets, then the glare of the camera flashes blinded me entirely.

I sold my name and face for a million projects and products. T-shirts and breakfast cereal, the puffed corn in the shape of my initial, M, with marshmallow space capsules for my lost brother. A microphone was jammed into my face as the hands of a million people tore at my clothes. I screamed, "I'm lost, I'm lost," and hit the asphalt.

Two and a half minutes later, Times Square was alive with the staccato beats of the latest dance hit, with my "I'm lost, I'm lost" digitized, warped and stripped of my own voice and emotion. It was pretty catchy, it stuck in the head. My friend Lisa pushed her way through the screaming twelve-year-olds to offer me the *hors d'oeurvs* from her tray. She wore the formal suit and tie I wore just seven minutes before. She peered up at me and smiles congratulations, but only for a moment. She knew the rules, she could only approach me, wordless and respectful or scream my name and fling her underwear at me. I slipped a small quiche into my mouth, but instead of swallowing, spit it out. The arms reached out and grabbed me around my waist, dragging me away to the stage.

"Good luck," Lisa called out to me, breaking the rules, "congratulations!"

They were all before me now. I had always said when it was time for my fifteen minutes, I knew exactly where I would look as I sang my song, or danced, or told my joke, or exposed my genitals. So I peered out over the sea of limbs and howling faces to the spot on a nearby corner where I used to stand, feet precariously balanced, fist pumping in the air. Someone was there, I could see a flash of blue, a shirt, maybe jeans? But whoever was standing there was just a blur. I tried to make out somebody's face, but even the people in the front row, the ones crushed against the stage, they were all screaming mouth or semiconscious swoon. So I just stared at the microphone and spoke.

"Thank you, thank you all for your support. My brother, I'm sure, feels your love, the way I do now. I never wanted my fifteen minutes of fame to start this way, with my only living relative trapped in a space capsule, unable to land. I just wish that each and every one of us will take a deep breath, right now, just one breath. And I pray to God above," and this point I gestured upward at a giant holographic antidepressant tablet beamed onto a cloud, "that our love just gives him one more breath for each person here tonight!" The crowd cheered. I looked at the clock. Five minutes left. Time for meaningless sex and cocaine. I dove into the crowd and let the carpet of arms embrace me and drag me down.

It was a crippled old peasant woman, swathed in colorful scarves, who brought me lines of the purest cocaine on a silver tray. "Peruvian," one of my handlers whispered to me, "the woman, the coke, the silver, all of it. Part of our New Realism campaign."

"Who are you?" I asked, turning my head, but my handler (they slide through the crowds, anointing and prodding those whose turn it is) had already melded back into the wall of people. I took the tray into my hands and watched the peasant woman right herself as I snorted. She swayed and stripped, dancing out of her indigenous clothing and tearing off the latex wrinkles, to show off her perfect young body, the best that money, my money could buy. I forgot my brother's name.

Three minutes. A game show, a quick memoir, maybe recording another sentence for posterity, I didn't want to go back to work yet. It is pure tedium in the factories, whether you're sewing the sequins onto a gown or making snacks, or in charge of building guitars to be smashed. The police have it slightly better, they get to choose where they stand in the perpetual party economy, but they don't get their fifteen minutes of fame until they beat down or shoot the wrong person. The handlers, well, nobody knows where they come from, but they have to be making a mint. I'd tell Lisa, back when we were equals, that I thought that handlers arranged the whole thing, that they were the only ones who got a piece of all the action. They got a piece of everyone's fifteen minutes, the food concessions, the factories, the travel and the ads that color the dome of night. They even get to tax us all to pay for the sweeping up every morning, while we work to make sure the party goes on.

And then Lisa would tell me, "At least we're white. The Third Worlders only get their fame when the handlers decide to stage a war party. I don't want my fifteen minutes to come from being dug out of a mass grave." She was always so straightforward. I found it harder to shove the broiled weenies into the dough when she'd get like that, but then I would think of my fifteen minutes and feel better.

A man came up to me and punched me hard in the face to the light of a million flashbulbs. The image of me on the ground, bleeding from the nose, crying, was instantly beamed across the earth. The crowd shifted slightly as the man's own fifteen minutes began. A world of microphones wanted to know why he did it, why did he punch a man in his hour of need? And then wanted to know how I felt.

"No pain!" I said, still crazed from the noise, the drugs, and the smells of the party economy. "No pain!" I said, rising to my feet. "No pain!" I pumped my fist in the air, and thousands followed my lead, proving that there was no pain with razors and syringes and cigarettes extinguished into arms, thighs and necks. There was pain though. I had one minute left. One minute left, then my world would end again. "Who to lay, what to say, was there time for another song or another t-shirt with my name, or is this an end game?" I said aloud, mostly to myself.

"Hey, you're a poet, nice," said a young woman with a tape recorder. She hit stop. And as she walked away, ignoring me like I was a ghost or a peasant, I knew my fame was over.

Some time later. The same day, the next? I was on the assembly line again, making four cents for each cocktail I wrapped in dough. Lisa was next to me.

"Your brother," she said slowly, "still has thirty seconds left. Your fame overshadowed his for a few minutes, but I've always been a fan of astronauts. I've been following him on the news."

"He was very brave," I said, sounding like the assembly line. It was a lockstep response. I didn't want to think about my time at the top anymore. Just let me work, let some master tell me how to move, how to shave a precious half-second from my technique, so that I can make a few more pigs in blankets every day.

"You should watch the tv," Lisa said, nodding up towards it. The factory had televisions over every work station, all the factories did. You could tell who had been famous, and who had not. The obscure watched while they worked, people like me spent their day staring at their hands instead. I looked up though and my brother was on, weightless, still alive, but gaunt and bearded.

"Hello America, hello world. This is Commander M of the spacecraft Nike. I've come to a decision. As you all know, I lost radio contact at 0900 hours, Swatch Time. The radiation that caused the system breakdown finally abated, and I'm able to communicate with you all. There are still too many malfunctions, I will not be able to return to earth, but I have made a decision."

I knew what the decision was. After all, he had a few seconds left.

"I have asked for and received clearance to leave orbit. I will head towards deep space and spend the rest of my time, until the oxygen on the Nike runs out, watching television signals transmitted into deep space. My own liftoff, sitcoms, who knows," he said, winking back a tear, "maybe I'll even be able to watch an old World Series game, one I missed as a kid. Is there a better way to die, than surrounded by the memories you love? Nike, after all, was the ancient Greek goddess of victory, and the end of this mission will be a victory to us all."

I turned to Lisa, but couldn't catch her eye. She was teletranced, in communion with my brother. She wanted to be up there too, watching old television commercials, listening to the hit songs and jingles we remembered as kids, without having to worry about anything else, not even the quickly fading oxygen supply. We all did. I turned away from the television and went back to work.

Brother Theodore Is Dead

Brother Theodore was always a ghost to me. When I returned to Manhattan in the early 1990s, Theodore was a specter haunting downtown. His one-man show, terrible and comic all at once, was still running on 13th Street, and posters boosting the show were everywhere. I saw them at the buildings at the New School For Social Research (dead, reborn as New School University), fluttering on lamp posts like wounded birds, shoved into Learning Annex and *New York Press* newsboxes, and slid under the door of my creaky railroad apartment on West 12th Street. He looked young in the posters, or the cartoonish profile of him did—he was half Charles Addams' Lurch, half Hanna Barbara's Magilla Gorilla. He was firmament and ephemera both, like the old dead bastards named Astor and Varick and Stuyvesant who pollute this city, like the vanished Indian trails that still make us veer west off Broadway. Everyone knew the Brother Theodore phenomenon, but nobody spoke about it, much the same way nobody spoke of Peter Stuyvesant even as they trampled upon and puked on the boundary of his old farm—The Bowery.

I finally saw the show, one of the final performances. Theodore was shorter than I expected, and much older too. I hadn't realized that the Holocaust survivor thing wasn't a gimmick, I hadn't realized that Theodore wasn't a character played by some pot-bellied trustfundian with a day job busing tables at Time Cafe. I was too young for Mike Douglas, and could never bear to sit through Letterman. I saw *The 'Burbs* and even the animated *The Last Unicorn*, but never connected name to voice or to face.

Theodore was dead then too, when he had his show. He was animated by cthonic forces, by the black ooze under Manhattan that takes care of its own. But he was damn funny, and he challenged the audience constantly. How dare we laugh at his pain, at all our pain, but we sure as hell shouldn't cry or whimper. My laughter was the nervous titter of someone absolutely sure that cemeteries aren't haunted or scary or dangerous. But Theodore led us out of the darkness again, by the end, and left to think about life and death. Dance till your legs rot off.

I wanted to see the show again, but nobody would come with me, and I didn't want to be one of those weirdoes who attended the show alone, over and over. Eventually, it closed, and Theodore faded into history. He was dead, I thought, as dead as the mice I trapped with glue and flung against walls in my Rivington Street slum, as dead as my friend Jay (from smack), as dead as my career plans to take the world of independent motion pictures by storm. I found myself on Long Island, writing term papers for wealthy but stupid college students, and then in Jersey City, doing the same.

Richard Metzger reintroduced me to Theodore. I had just volunteered myself as a writer for Disinfo.com, and Richard invited me to cross the Hudson (but not in the form of a beautiful swan, the way Theodore himself did, every day, at 2PM) and come out to lunch. He was a friend of Theodore's, who was inexplicably still alive, but in constant pain and unable to leave his apartment. I could interview him, Richard said, and give the old man a little company to break up the monotony of his life. Theodore was going deaf, he couldn't watch television. He couldn't visit with his friends, who were all much younger than him (even his girlfriend was half his age, in her forties), and he couldn't even fall asleep without pain.

So I went. Theodore was hilarious as long as I sat on his right side, where he could still hear me. Sharp as a whip. Strong as a suspension bridge, even in his nineties. His arms were like tensile steel wrapped in a netting of pork fat. Whatever dark trades he had made earlier in his life offered him some vitality to go along with the imprisonment and pain of his final days. I couldn't interview him with Richard there, though, he said, I'd have to come back. He'd get another evening of company out of me that way, but I was glad to do it, deadlines be damned.

So I went back. It took him two minutes to walk across his efficiency apartment to answer the door. He smiled a crooked, gaping headwound smile, and invited me in. He told me everything. How Einstein visited his home as a child, and how the scientist answered profound dinner-time questions about God and the nature of the cosmos with, "How the hell would I know?" Young Theodore played chess with Einstein during that time. "He was a very mediocre chess player," Theodore told me, "much like yourself."

Theodore used to hustle chess in the park. He was a member of a local club when in his prime, and regularly lost money to the Grandmasters when depressed (Grandmasters only play for money) but collected pieces and pawns like stamps otherwise. I am a good enough player to know how bad I am. The one-move-at-a-time ducks were easy pickins', but anyone who thinks more than three moves ahead gets my queen in no time. Thus, I never played with anyone—there would be no point to it, since I would either win easily or lose utterly. I played the computer though, time and again, and erased my games afterwards, just in case Deep Blue gained sentience and hacked into my box for a larf. But I played Theodore, because there are things one does for old men that one does for nobody else.

Theodore was still an excellent chess player, but his brain was dying. He had a great number of opening moves, but senility and pain kept his head out of the game. We drew a few, he won a few, I won once. I think he let me, to keep me interested, to keep me coming back.

He asked me about me. I told him that I used to live with a woman who was also in constant pain, thanks to childhood sexual and physical abuse. He wept, saying that he couldn't bear to feel sorry for himself and his situation when there are young people whose bodies were broken in the same way his was after nearly a century of living. This, from a man who faced Dachau. I wanted to hug him, but I felt I'd break him.

I visited him a couple of times after that as well, for chess and takeout food. He grew more distant, as his personality began to collapse into senility, senility exacerbated by constant agony (try to think and be witty with your limbs in thick vices) and near-complete deafness. He called me a few times, to ask about his appearance on Disinfo's tv show. Was he still funny? Yes. Compelling? Yes. Did the audience at Disinfo Con like his little video? They loved it. Would he get his $800? Beats me, I told him, I just write about George W. Bush and people who like to fuck stuffed animals for Disinfo, I have nothing to do with the tv show or the money. He told me I speak too fast (I do) and that I shouldn't torture him by rambling on the phone when he wants to speak with me (I'm sorry).

On my twenty-eighth birthday, which I spent alone in the former crackhouse I had recently bought, he called me again. He was very far gone. Theodore couldn't remember my name, but he somehow remembered that February twentieth was my birth date. He knew that I was a friend of Richard's (sure) a playwright (not) and "devastatingly handsome" (. . . uhm). Would I come and see him again soon? Yes, maybe. Did we play chess once? We did, a number of times. Was I that terrible player he kept beating? Oh yes.

I never saw Theodore after that. I couldn't bear it. My visits with him were draining, like watching three thousand years worth of crumbling pyramids in an instant. I tried to keep track of him, from afar. He had an advice-for-the-lovelorn column for *Mean Magazine.* That meant that somebody must be visiting him, to read him letters and record his responses, right? Good, good. I asked Richard for Theodore's number again, in April of 2000, but never called it.

I even thought about writing this appreciation, even though I barely knew Theodore (and I thought about writing this parenthetical comment, to explain that I thought about writing that I thought about writing this appreciation (and this one as well (and this one, on and on, into the dark pit of nothingness at the center of existence))) and didn't know much about his life, other than what he told me.

He told me that Gil Hodges' widow often saw Gil's ghost, and that he hoped people had breasts and buttocks and cocks in heaven. He distrusted his senses and their limitations, even before they began to betray him. Once, he saw Woody Allen on tv, in some film he couldn't remember, and saw the most exquisite moment of acting as Allen's character looked on at a wedding he wasn't a part of. A look, not a pose or an expression, captured the essence of experience in a way that no other actor he could. Theodore didn't like his role in *The Last Unicorn,* because he couldn't be himself. He didn't hope to die on stage, but he wouldn't have minded if that's how it happened. He never voted, except in Screen Actors' Guild elections. He hoped that one day someone would do something with a short film in the German Expressionist style he had made forty-five years ago, *Midnight Café*. And he was disappointed that I didn't share his enthusiasm for dancing till one's legs rotted off, for truly living only when one was mere steps from the mouth of the grave.

I was disappointed in myself too, I still am, for not seeing Theodore more often, for not wanting a larger share of the dead heat of his collapsing dwarf star, for not thinking and joking and firing my synapses till they collapsed into gray jelly in a cold skull. I deleted the chess game from my computer, and emptied the recycle bin tonight. I'll never play chess again.

April 16th, 2001.

Time of Day

I had just gotten off work and was on my way to more work when the phones in my mind rang. It was another seven jobs calling in, begging for my attention. In headspace, my ego agent, a slick and well-tanned Victor Mature, arranged them according to potential economic gain, neo-Marxist need measurement, and location.

I stuck my coffee cup in the beverage holder and leaned heavily on the wheel. Traffic was snarled. I initiated my patented anti-traffic protocol: "Whoo, let's go!" I shouted. I even banged my hands on the dashboard, but the snaking lines of red lights between me and my gig weren't impressed. I rewarded myself with more coffee anyway.

In headspace, my homunculus—a small, gray-winged gargoyle—shook its fist at the car ahead of me. My ego agent handed me his travelling salesman recommendation, a crazed zigzag all over the tri-state. His plan was the cheapest and quickest way to install all the jacks, but my wetnurse was pinging about my pulse rate, lung color, and electrolyte levels, so I did my own math. I took two seconds to read a short article about another week of the Brown Haze over the city and decided that I needed a vacation. I'd do only one jackgig. A whole day spent on only one job instead of my usual eleven jobs a day. Far away. A monastery upstate, Greek Orthodox even. A vacation, or as close to one as jacked employees get.

The country would be quiet and the sky large. Like the parking lot I pulled into, but even bigger and with less soot.

"Okay, here we all are," I said to the kids. Not all my gigs were high-paying and glamorous; I was leading a tour of corporate HQ that night. Hi, I am Kelly Angelakis and I picked the short straw. Pleased to meet ya.

The kids gathered by the large office windows and stared up at me. They were college sophomores—the oldest was probably thirteen—and their eyes were wide and white, their skin slick with sweat. Their adrenal patches, all but mandatory for people on the go these days, were doing a bit too much to their young bodies. Some of the girls were almost vibrating in their sneakers. My ego agent provided me with some magnetizdat oral histories of patch addiction, but they were interrupted and replaced by soothing propaganda designed to reassure me. And I got some crossthought from another jack.

("Jesus forgive me, a miserable sinner!")

I sent the homunculus winging into the dark corners of my headspace to find the source of the crossthought, but he flew back to me empty-handed. Whoever was murmuring that little ditty needed a vacation worse than I did. Was it Sam, up on level seven? He was a pervert or something, and frequently filled nearby jacks with crapthink.

I couldn't bear to make eye contact with the tour group for more than a few seconds at a time, so I kept glancing out the window at the bright cityscape. The sky was black and the moon obscured by fog; more Brown Haze for tomorrow. A snarl of blinking red and white lights from the day's fifth rush hour entranced me for a second, but the sound of ten people twitching woke me up. I couldn't get a tenthsecond's rest that night.

My homunculus went and found that errant bit of religious crossthink: it came from the jackgig request up at the monastery. A distraction. Victor Mature stepped up to the mic to take over the tour.

(Stock footage of Bill Cosby entered from skull-right and accepted a cigar from Freud with a smile. "Some acumen agents may appear as imaginary friends." A human-sized cartoon cigar with flickering red ash for hair, goggle eyes rolling and stick-figure limbs akimbo, marched into view and waved. The crowd giggled as if on cue.)

In headspace, the homunculus flew into view and unfurled a parchment. A green visor hung from its horns and it waved a quill pen in one claw. Cute. My helicopter to the country was ready. I blinked my signature at the parchment and the image derezzed.

The children were all quivering eyes and hair slicked down against clammy skin (—delete that, only happythink tonight!). Victor gave the standard disclaimer, pointed out the gift shop and cheerily spat out the company slogan, "We're Not Just Jack."

(Corporate logo, cue jingle.)

The helicopter was still ready, and I was already late. There was no way the elevator would get me to the roof on time. In headspace, My Pet Dog scuttled forward and stared at the copter's scheduling systems with his puppy-dog eyes. He scored twenty seconds for me. I took the steps up to the roof three at a time, swallowed a lungful of whipping smog on the helipad and hopped aboard.

(My Pet Dog was a droopy old basset hound with folds of brown and white fur draped over his snout. Designed to curry favor with acumen and humans alike, he almost never failed. Even a helicopter had to submit to his cuteness.)

"Are you well rested, or just patched?" the pilot asked. He was old and had that skinny-guy-with-a-paunch look that ex-athletes and the unpatched had. I didn't know his name or number, so I couldn't look him up on the jacknet. Small talk. Grr.

"I'm patched," I said, trying to sound a bit apologetic. "That's business, you know, a working girl has to make a living." He smiled when I said "working girl." What a Neanderthal. My Pet Dog had already sniffed out his body language and idiolect, cross-referenced it with his career choice, and suggested a conversational thread.

I looked out the window. "Shame, isn't it?" I knew he'd know I was talking about the smog.

"The Brown Haze. Have you ever seen a white cloud? I know you live in the city."

"Sure I've seen them, in the country. Won't there be some over the hills by the monastery?"

He nodded once, as people of his temperament tend to. "Yeah."

Then I realized that I was only hearing him with my ears. He wasn't jacked at all. He'd just waited for me instead of overriding his helicopter and taking off without me. He'd done—what was it?—a favor.

It was hot in the cockpit, too hot, and my connection to the net faded. Victor Mature was beginning to warble, but the wetnurse rushed up and gave me a shot of sleepytime before my jack overheated entirely. Snoozeville.

"Excuse me, I only had three seconds of the language," I said in heavily accented Greek. The monk just smiled, showing that he actually had a pair of lips under his thick black beard. It was quiet outside, and cold.

"Welcome to Saint Basil's," he said in the bland English of disk jockeys and foreigners who've had their accents eradicated. "I'm Brother Peter." He smiled weakly, his lips still moving slightly, like he was talking to himself. Or like he had just had a jack installed. ("It is two thirty five ay em," the homunculus whispered.) The monastery was impressive from the outside, at least: a squat four-story building made of thick carved granite. The lawn was well-kept, but still a bit wild, with weeds and poorly pruned brushes lining the walkway up the hill. I heard some crickets chirping away in soothing unison. It reminded me of the city, but quieter, like the volume was turned down on the universe. The noise of the jacknet was far away too, like waves lapping a shoreline just out of sight.

"My God, you're tired." I looked him over but couldn't see any of the telltale sweat or twitches. My own patches responded to that stray thought with another surge of tingly chemicals to the bloodstream. I blinked hard and rose to the tips of my toes. "I'm sorry, I'm . . . you know . . . I am not used to people who . . . actually let themselves get tired."

"People who are not from the city," Peter said. He didn't smile this time, but he muttered something to himself after he spoke, then bowed his head slightly and took a step backward. "Come in, please."

I slipped through the door and frowned. The walls were plain old drywall, with an icon or two hanging from nails for decoration. The ceiling lights were old yellow incandescent bulbs, and the monastery's little foyer smelled of wax, incense, and unwashed feet. I got another burst of crossthought. (" . . . have mercy on me, a miserable sinner.")

The source was here, somewhere down below. I could feel a jack pinging nearby, a strange chanting beat. There was only one of them, though, not the thousands I was used to in the city. Like one water droplet falling into a still puddle, it stood out.

Even out in the real world, it was quiet. Wind moved over the grass. Peter tugged on the sleeve of my blouse.

"Ms. Angelakis, you'll need to retire for several hours at least. Morning prayers are in ninety minutes. Then we hold a morning liturgy, and of course—"

"Women may not attend the liturgy. After the morning meal, we will meet again so we may begin my examination of George Proios, who needs a jack installed," I said along with him. There were only two variances. Peter said "your examination" instead of "my examination," which I expected. More importantly, he said "removed" instead of "installed." And his lips moved even after he finished speaking.

"What? Why would he want his jack removed?" I asked, my voice spiking enough to make My Pet Dog wince. My ego agent immediately got FedEx on the jacknet and had them send my tools out. "I wasn't told this was a removal. A removal requires tools and facilities that I do not have. A removal needs a medical doctor. I'm just an installer. Assembly-line stuff. I'm unskilled labor."

"Brother George does not want his jack removed. However, he requires it. We require it. He is a medical doctor and can assist you in that regard. He believes he can work with you, which is why he requested you."

In the headspace, I ran to one of the phones and hit the hot button, but there was no dial tone.

The inky blackness of my headspace solidified into a curved stone wall, a cave with no entrance or exit. The homunculus tried to fly to the shadows, to the open networks, but slammed against the mental block and fell at my feet, twitching. The wetnurse knelt down to repair it. Outside, I was still, staring off into space.

"Ms. Angelakis?" Peter asked. He waved his hand in front of my face.

I stepped back up, my vision refocusing on the outside world. Peter's lips twitched silently. I wanted to rip his beard off, to feel the wiry hair in my hands, but the wetnurse sedated me. From a few feet under the floor, I felt George Proios's malfunctioning jack repeating one recursive command, one thought, over and over. In the corner of my headspace, I sensed him, like an old file I'd forgotten to delete, like a shadow on a cave wall.

("Step up, there's a world out there!" Victor Mature demanded. Kelly snapped to attention.)

"He's having his jack removed," I said to Peter. "How can he assist me?" The wetnurse ran about my headspace with cold compresses, but I got all flushed anyway. I could feel the heat pouring from my skin. Peter's expression didn't change; his eyes were distant and his body still but for his twitching lips.

"You do not need his help, just his consent," he said, finally. His voice retained that dreamy, flat tone, like a computer or a jazz radio announcer.

"Jesus forgive me!" I said. "I'm not going to break half a dozen laws and risk a man's . . . " I stopped and realized what I had just said.

(The homunculus flew about Kelly's head, a flashing red siren strapped to its head. "Warning, warning," it screeched. Kelly waved it away.)

Peter didn't smile. I licked a line of sweat off my top lip. In the headspace, My Pet Dog went sniffing after shadows. Downstairs, he was in a basement cell: George Proios. One command line, one task endlessly replicated by his Sinner Self, the Holy Spirit, and A Young Lamb, the monk's custom acumen agents. Some religious people even installed Jesus Christ masques, to keep them from fucking strange women or swearing. I'd never seen anyone with a lamb before. Certainly not one standing alongside a dove bathed in nearly blinding light and a haggard, leprous monk who was mindlessly repeating "O Lord Jesus Christ, Son of God, Jesus forgive me, a miserable sinner." My homunculus slapped its little claw against its forehead ("We could have had a V8!"). Then the monk turned to me, staring with his dead eyes, and linked our jacks. The shadow on the cave wall of my headspace began to murmur a prayer. *Jesus forgive me, a miserable sinner, so I won't have to think anymore.*

(Kelly Angelakis, age fourteen. She was thin and underdeveloped, with a huge mop of black curls splayed on the pillows. Her palm ran over her nude stomach, sliding down between her legs. Then guilt and bitter vomit filled her mouth.)

"I am sure you will help him, Ms. Angelakis. Brother George assures us that you are a good Greek girl. Also, he tells us that the state he is experiencing is . . . how would one put it . . . contagious, no?" He turned on his heel and led me to my room. I glanced up at the back of his neck, just to make sure. Smooth skin and wiry black hair. No jack.

They were all dry here. I could only sense one other signal, the drumbeat of George Proios and his begging cybernetic prayer. It overwhelmed his system and hit mine hard too. The homunculus scratched at headspace's new walls, trying to get out, but it was grounded. I was cut off from the network now, thanks to distance, granite, and the white noise chant of "Jesus forgive me." He had trapped me. The last message he'd allowed out was for the equipment I needed.

In the headspace, Victor Mature stepped into view. "Kelly, listen. We can get through this. Don't forget how good you are. Proios sounds dangerous, but he's going to let you knock him out and uninstall his jack. We can do it and then we'll be able to call the police, the sysops, the FBI. All we have to do is take it easy for a few hours, do a job just like we were planning, and then we can leave. And all we need to do to succeed is not fall apart right now." I opened my mouth to answer him like he was standing next to me, then caught myself.

(My Pet Dog whimpered, knowing that even if the company was interested in Kelly's location, it would be cheaper to hire some thirteen-year-old right out of college to replace her than to waste the copter fuel on retrieving her. Kids worked more cheaply and had a useful decade in them before burning out. And everyone was too busy to worry about Kelly or where she was anyway.)

My room was spartan, with blank walls, a cot, and a small table where a candle, a Bible, and a bunch of grapes were laid out for me. A water cooler bubbled to itself on the opposite end of the room. My wetnurse suggested flipping though the New Testament, "purely to keep our mind on something else right now." I hadn't read a whole book in years, hadn't needed to. I flipped through the pages and ran my palms over the vellum, and quickly sliced my finger open on the gold leaf of a page from *Revelations*. I sucked on my finger for a few seconds, then decided to try something else. Being alone, without the net, was . . . disconcerting. Hell, it was scary.

I thought I'd to make a game of seeing how far I could spit grape seeds, but the grapes were seedless. I stretched out on the bed—the mattress was hard and lumpy—and closed my eyes. In the headspace, my ego agent brought out the old film projector and suggested a movie. I shrugged and pulled down the screen.

(Victor Mature took his place in front of the projection screen, the cave morphing about him into a Hollywood studio. My Pet Dog jumped into his arms and licked his face, "Oh, Won Ton Ton," the ego agent crooned, "you'll be perfect!" "Yeah, Nick, he sure will be!" someone called from offscreen.)

I squeezed my eyes shut tighter. I'd already seen this movie too many times. *Won Ton Ton, the Dog Who Saved Hollywood,* a cheesy bit of tinsel that I'd caught on television at three in the morning once, when I was seven. Victor Mature had played Nick. I was so happy to hear my father's name on TV. It was either Victor Mature or Santa Claus, so I glommed onto Victor.

George Proios was still in my mind. He dug through my memories like someone picking through a bowl of pistachios.

(Kelly Angelakis, age seven. Nick Angelakis towered over her, a torn book in his hand, the pages falling around Kelly like feathers from a burst pillow. "Why do you read this garbage! This is for retarded kids, Kalliope, with the space ships and pointy ears. What is he supposed to be,"—the back of the hand slapped the cover of the novel—"the devil?"

From the kitchen, Vasso Angelakis called out "Leave her alone, let her read what she wants!"

"I'm trying to raise my daughter right!" Nick shouted back.)

Childhood was another movie I had seen too many times already. I took a deep breath, pulled myself up out of bed, and hit the hallway. Peter was waiting for me, his eyes wide with confusion, his lips still going, and a package in his hands.

"Ms. Angelakis?"

"Come on, let's go see Proios now. He's doing . . . something."

"What?"

" . . . Praying!"

"Well, yes, I certainly hope so," Peter said, glancing out one of the dark windows in the hallway. "It has been only four minutes since I showed you the room. Please try to get some rest. I brought you blankets.

I'll come for you after morning prayers. I'm sure your mail will be here by then."

There was no threat in his tone or body language, but I took a backward step into the room anyway. Then he said, "Will you need more blankets?"

"No, I'm fine." I closed the door. Goddamn, I needed to turn off my head, but Proios was digging through my old files. He introduced a virus into my headspace, one smarter than my wetnurse— an artificial mental illness called existential angst. Bastard.

(Kelly Angelakis, age seventeen. The back of her head was shaved. Her father, now an inch shorter than she, shook his head slowly as she explained, "I can talk to people with it, access information. Everyone's going to have one, one of these days, just like the computer."

"I never used the computer," Nick Angelakis said. "This is terrible. You want to talk to people? You can talk to me, you can talk to Mama, your friends in school. You should have learned Greek, if you wanted to talk to people. Your poor grandmother can't say two words to you.")

My eyes refocused from the blank walls of my headspace to the blank walls of the room. I decided that I would lie still and be perfectly silent, to listen to the building. That lasted two seconds. The homunculus flung itself against the headspace's cave walls again. Back to the grapes, this time making a game of how many I could fit into my mouth at once (fifteen!) but I started gagging and had to dig a few of them out of my mouth and crush the rest by pushing on my cheeks with my palms.

I had already used up my sleepytime with that damn nap on the helicopter. I counted the beats of a cricket chirping and then counted the holes in the ceiling tiles. One hundred and eighty-five holes per tile, thirty-eight tiles. Seven thousand and thirty ceiling tile holes in this room. The dimensions of the room and layout of the hallway suggested eight rooms of identical size on this floor. Was it dawn yet? Fifty-six thousand, two hundred and forty holes in the ceiling tiles on this floor. How many floors? Four.

Was it dawn yet? ("It is three fifteen ay em," the homunculus whispered.) Random facts littered headspace. Saint Nicholas (there's that name again) was the patron saint of Greece and of sailors. "And of prostitutes," the shadow on the cave wall whispered. Only twenty percent of the land in Greece is arable, while nearly ninety-two percent of Greece's population lives near the endless coastlines. (Jesus forgive me.)

I had been to church once, years ago, after my father died. It was a blur now, thanks to my jack and my busy little brain. The priest was mumbling in Greek and my jack was off, at mother's request—three hours of processing time I'll never get back. No translation but the priest's own, which was incomplete. The line "Life is more elusive than a dream" was the only thing I remembered from the sermon. I haven't dreamed in eight years.

The night before my father—not Dad, not Papa—died, I slept with a boy named Thomas Smith. My Pet Dog dug a hole at my feet and found the old sensations, the breeze on my back, the moisture, the throbbing in my tired calves after a few minutes of squelching. Was it dawn yet? That's all I wanted to know then, and all I wanted to know now. It wasn't, though. ("It's three forty seven ay em," the homunculus whispered.) I gave up, closed my eyes, and actually, really, naturally slept. And I dreamed. I was taking a final exam after cutting class all semester. I was naked.

I awoke to a knock on the door, and was up in point two seconds. Brother Peter and I slipped past half a dozen other monks. Their footfalls were quiet enough, but it wasn't the sound of six dryboys, it was the lockstep beat of a jacked workplace. And the murmuring, the lips, each man I passed was muttering to himself. I glanced at the backs of their necks as they passed, but there were no jacks to be seen. Dry as a bone, and dry to the bone. But every one of them was tied to some jacknet, somewhere.

Peter had my FedEx package tucked under his arm and was marching down the hall, sending the hem of his cassock flying up to his knees. I was faster, though, and kept stepping on his heels.

"Brother Peter," I said, "you do realize, of course, that when I get back to the city, I'm going to put you on report. Not just for demanding this highly irregular removal, but for kidnapping me! This is contract under false pretenses, this is misallocation of processing time, this is wire fraud—"

"Please help him." He handed me the package and nodded towards a flight of steps leading down into a basement. "Go on."

"You're not coming with me?" I asked him. "How can I trust you on any of this? Heck, how can you trust me, I can go down there and lobotomize him." Peter shrugged and mumbled something again. In headspace, I heard Proios's own voice chanting, "O Lord Jesus Christ, Son of God, Jesus forgive me, a miserable sinner." The ego agent joined in the chant, in Victor Mature's dusky tones. My Pet Dog howled.

Then I realized that Peter hadn't been mumbling to himself. He had been reciting the same prayer as George, the same as the six other monks marching down the hall. The homunculus perched on my shoulder and held out a headspace lantern. In the real world, my pupils instantly adjusted to the dark and I walked down the steps.

George Proios looked just like the monk I had seen in the crossthought, and his shadow was splayed against the stone wall of the basement, just like it was in my headspace. His beard was long and matted, held against his chest by his own sweat and grime. He smiled.

("Jesus forgive me," the wetnurse muttered, and performed a preliminary diagnosis on our subject).

His lips weren't moving. I realized then that mine were. That upstairs, Peter's still were. That every monk was saying a little prayer. They were always saying a little prayer. Now I was too, I was on a new jacknet. Except there was no jack necessary, and no net.

"Have you found God?" George asked.

"I'm here to remove your jack."

He didn't say anything for a long moment. Then he nodded towards a small table. A slice of bread sat there, not doing much. The words "Have you eaten?" came from somewhere—headspace or real world, I didn't know. He rose up and shuffled towards the table, split the piece in half and offered it to me. I looked down and my face flushed. I held a complete piece of bread in my hand, and George still had a full slice in his hand. "More?" He broke his piece in two again and offered me one of them. It was cold and heavy in my hand. The slice was whole, though, and now I had two pieces of bread. Two whole pieces of bread.

"I would like to remove the jack, and then leave," I said. I dropped the bread on the floor and took a step forward, My Pet Dog feeding me a conversational thread of icy professionalism designed to engender compliance.

"I have no wish for the jack to be removed," he said.

"It's broken. Malfunctioning. You're experiencing a severe cognitive loop, probably because of a physical defect in the jack's antenna array. I can't do a spinal intervention here, but without reception, your problem should alleviate itself," My Pet Dog said to me and I said to George.

George shrugged. "I do not have a problem. I pray without ceasing, as Scripture demands. I do what my brothers spend their adult lives attempting through privation and contemplation. One begins by praying as often as one can, on the level of the spoken word. All the time, one must begin to pray, muttering, whispering, thinking. Finally, after long years one can literally pray without ceasing. One's thoughts are always with God, not with sin. I pray from the heart, not from the jack. I am serene." My Pet Dog opened the package and spread the instruments on the tabletop.

"Look," George said, grabbing the two pieces of bread from the table. "Look! How do you explain this? Science, no? Somehow? What, with your quantum something-or-other?" He waved his arms and shoved the bread under my nose. Spittle coated his beard, and his arms were as thin as twigs. With a conductor's flourish, he whipped the sleeves of his robe up to his elbows and threw the bread on the ground. I took a step forward. "Mesmerism, perhaps, no? My jack interfering with yours? Have you thought of sin this morning, my child? Are you at peace? Have you ever even breathed? Jesus have mercy on me, a miserable sinner. Jesus have mercy on you."

George knelt to the floor near my feet, his head near the bread. The Jesus Prayer had done it. Two pieces where there used to be one. The dusty crusts, my footprint impressed onto one of them, existed. Without having to buy or sell them, without eleven jobs to pay for them, without a jingle. A miracle, at my feet.

I slapped a patch on George's neck and he dropped like a few sticks wrapped in a rag. Maybe I could know God after all. No more existential angst, no more rushing from job to job, the fabled free lunch. The bread. I tapped into George's spine and began to draw the information from him. The inspiration from him. It was like breathing a rainbow, but I could taste bread and wine, flesh and blood, in my mouth.

("The Lord tells us in Thessalonians 5:17 to 'Pray without ceasing,'"

George explained to Kelly. "Our brothers have spent their lives contemplating their navels, muttering the words to themselves, trying to never lose contact with God. But I couldn't. The world was too distracting, too earnest. So I had a pirate jack installed, and found a way. And I prayed so well that God allowed others to hear me as well."

It was world of the Godnet: all the jackless wonders out there with one job, one personality, and one little life each, the whole smelly superstitious lot of them. And now Kelly was jacked in too.)

With George unconscious and his netblock gone, the rest of yesterday's junkmail finally downloaded and hit my brain. The latest news, spinning into headspace like a shot of a newspaper in an old movie, let me know what I had been missing for the past few hours. War with the Midwest, wethead bias crimes against dryboys on the rise, sumo results, the GM workers' council calling for a strike, markets down. People had things to buy and sell, important pinhead opinions to howl across my brain. I was needed, necessary, a crucial memebucket for the best the world had to offer, at low low interest rates. No thanks, I thought to myself (to myself, not some nano-neurological stooge!); I quit.

In headspace, I shot My Pet Dog. I shot him dead, and took over my body, once and for all.

Headspace crumbled and a noisy blackness buried me. I think I fell to my knees, or was it on my face? I couldn't breathe. My lips were clenched shut, but vomit poured into my mouth and through the gaps in my teeth. Then, in headspace, I felt the firm hand of my ego agent on the back of my neck, lifting me above the swirling advertisements, the dizzying dance of thousands of stock prices, and the casual emergencies of work and memos and updated job queues. I coughed up the liquid shit of it all and finally, finally, took a moment. And I breathed, and my breath was a prayer.

I turned to face my acumen. The light from Victor Mature's miner's helmet dazzled my eyes, but that was probably just the jack's way of explaining the stars I saw from the bump on my head. The homunculus flew overhead, clutching My Pet Dog's corpse in his claws. The wetnurse was standing on a stepladder as a waist-deep flood of information spilled into our little world.

"Guess what, gang?" I said. "You're all fired. I don't need to work twenty-three point seven hours a day anymore, and neither does anyone else. God will provide." In headspace, I held up two pieces of miracle bread, and threw them to the floor. Then I fired my acumen agents. With my gun.

The jack removal took longer than I thought it would. The scalpel felt too heavy in my hands; my fingers were too stiff to move. My connection to the jacknet was a distant scream, like a child left behind in a parking lot by his deranged parents. George's eyes were still open, in spite of the narcotic. What would he be like when he woke up? Would he still be tied into the Godnet, like the monks upstairs? Like me? An overheated Jesus guided my hands, and my thoughts. His face was red, and steam poured from his ears.

The police took my ego agents' posthumous statements. (Damn backups.) I heard their filing cabinet drawer slam shut and echo. They'd get to my case by the time I was ninety, if I lived that long. My dry cleaning was done and the menu for the next three weeks needed to be planned; provisions needed to be requisitioned. My apartment back in the city wanted to know if it could please water the plants. A personal ad wrote itself for me and begged for my eyeblink signature. Sneaky anarchist magnetizdats nipped at my ankles, demanding attention. Helicopter blades were talking to me, saying "hurry hurry hurry" with the whip of wind. I had a deadline to meet. One deadline a second, every second, for the rest of my life.

("'Lord Jesus Christ, have mercy on me, a miserable sinner' is as powerful for its cadence as it is for its content. Once integrated into the head, it is actually hard to remove. Rather, one begins to receive, the monks say, messages from God," Kelly said, mimicking the sing-song of the prayer.)

I sent the jacknet a final, very important message, the same one George had sent me. *Jesus forgive me, a miserable sinner.* I reached behind my neck and blindly disconnected my jack. I was alone, but for the constant prayer on my lips and the love for every man and woman in the world. The Godnet.

I ate a sandwich and sat on the hill just outside the monastery, waiting for the helicopter. Everyone in the Godnet ate that sandwich, the two pieces of bread coming straight from George's miracle—after I brushed the dirt off of them, of course. And I tasted gyros in Cyprus, kimchi in Pyongyang, and injera in Addis Ababa. And I even felt the tickle of a patch here and exhaust-stained breakfast coffee there, from the first jacknetters to be infected with the God virus. Information wasn't a horrible flood of jingles and logos and unfair trades of wayward seconds of processing time any more; it was a smile, a wave, a breeze, a broken leg. Even the dying felt good, because there was always a birth right behind it.

It was odd, being alone, but not at all scary anymore. It was odd, being one with the world and everyone in it. It was hard, eating a sandwich and incessantly muttering the prayer at the same time. It was nice, though, to know that the Godnet would be giving me food and water and love and a place to live. Miracle bread for everyone. I heard angels' wings, but they were really only the spinning rotors of the copter.

The trip back. I spoke with the pilot. She had kids. She played the cello. She'd been raped once, at thirteen, but was healing now, and her lips moved with an invisible prayer. Her jack was cold and nearly dormant, buzzing with low-grade euphoria. We were just in range of the city, and I could already hear the Jesus Prayer—the God virus—in the ear of every poor jacked bastard in town. It was all prayer now; they shut down the news, the soaps, and even the ads. The reporters were too busy taking time off to report on the collapse of the economy, the wine flowing from the public urinals, the lame walking, the stupid finally getting a clue, the kids actually sleeping—really really sleeping and then getting up because it was morning, not because it was time for their shifts. As we flew down into the city, the sun rose into the already-shrinking pool of brown smog that sat atop the skyline like a bad toupee. Morning. Not work or betweenwork or morework. I knew what time of day it was.

Do the Wall Street Hustle

Being a bohemian Communist without a mutual fund, a 401(k), or any valueless dot com stocks to add to the oil drum fires the homeless gather around, I don't often find myself in the Financial District. But when I do, I get the biggest kick out of seeing white brokers, lawyers and computer guys lining up for the three-card monte games run by dusty-looking blacks, Latinos and Roma atop cardboard boxes. Full of blowhard confidence, these Wall Street gurus refuse to believe that the rest of us have already figured out. You can't win.

Three-card monte is a simple trick. The tosser holds up two black cards and one red one, and tosses them face down on a table. He shuffles them a bit, then asks the punter (in this case, one of the Wall Street guys) to point to the red card. Thanks to a little prestidigitation, the red card appears to have been dropped first, but was really dropped second. The punter loses the card's place and thus his money. Repeat till the cops arrive.

And on this sunny April afternoon, the cops were nowhere to be seen. I watched one guy dump $300 in six minutes and then leave with a smile on his face as two more fellows fell in after him and placed their bets. One of the guys—I'll call him Stan Laurel because he was a long stringbean of a man—dumped $75 in three turns. His pal, a hefty, sweating Oliver Hardy sort, was a bit smarter. So smart that he actually called the right card after Laurel eliminated one of the black cards with his incorrect guess. Hardy was so smart, in fact, that he fell into the tosser's second trap.

"One bet atta time, one bet atta time," the tosser said, then offered Hardy $100 a turn. Hardy ran out of money after two rounds. By the time the crowd started turning against the tosser, I had watched him pocket at least $800. Not bad for twenty minutes' work.

Three-card monte has been around since at least fifteenth-century Spain, and the even older shell game was probably played in the shadow of the pyramids. By the nineteenth century, tossers were dressed to the nines, playing on the image of the professional gambler. Tired and hungry settlers, half-drunk prospectors and bumpkins were their punters. Millions of hard lessons later, the unwary marks learned the basic lesson of capitalism: there ain't ever gonna be something for nothing. So they dropped out of the game, leaving only the wary.

But what makes the game such a powerful draw down in the Financial District? Even in these economic doldrums, the average Wall Street punter can still work through lunch and pocket more money working the phones than he ever could with a game of three-card monte. It's the nature of scam to tantalize, though. Working the phones is hard. Shaking down some poor sucker on the street, especially when he looks and acts like a laid-off janitor, seems easy in contrast. The money is flying. The sun is bright. The smell of boiled hot dogs is in the air. And there's no way some street guy can beat a polished financial predator, right?

Three-card monte now depends on what they call "the rube act." The tosser I observed was great. Rotten sneakers, holey jeans, worn T-shirt and a missing tooth. His entire ensemble could have been purchased ten times over for the price of one of his victim's neckties. Who could resist? Certainly not the Wall Street people. They think this guy must be running his game out of desperation, hoping that luck will put a few bucks in his pocket. The game seems simple. Get lucky and win! Even if you're unlucky, you've not lost that much, and there's always next round, right? But three-card monte isn't that simple.

The tosser's investment in human resources is quite extensive, for example. There's a shill, who appears to win the game; a roper, who attracts folks to the game and encourages people to play, muscle to settle disputes in the tosser's favor and a lookout to watch out for the fuzz.

What makes three-card monte so hilarious is that the scam is now so obvious. These days, even TV sitcoms debunk it. The police departments posts signs in subway stations to warn off the tourists, and the trick itself is easy enough to teach children. It's been dissected in books and magazines for years. Why play it then? Canada Bill Jones, the famous monte operator and Faro addict put it best.

"I know the game is crooked," he said once, while losing his shirt in a dirty Faro game, "but it's the only game in town."

May, 2002.

The Armory Show

Microrecorder, check. Contact lens camera with image reproduction licensing protocol, check. Tickets to the exhibit, check. Mace, check. Shiv, check. Tube sock, check. Can of Diet Coke, check. Good to go. The last two are an old trick of my mother's. Back when she was a social worker—back when there *was* such a thing—she'd occasionally end up cornered by a red-eyed rat, some crackbaby gone nuts or one of her own clients who boiled with rage when she came to tell them that there would be no more government cheese. Soda cans were usually waved past the metal detectors by the lobby guards and when it hit the fan, she'd just slide her can into the sock and start swinging till the fabric was scarlet with blood. She retired with four justifiable homicides and a full pension.

These days I need that kind of protection too. After all, I'm an art critic. I plan on surviving this night.

Tonight, the armory show opens. Yes, like the famous one of 1913, 175 years ago, back when Duchamp, Dasburg and the Cubist "Chamber Of Horrors" shocked the world by exhibiting paintings and sculptures depicting subjects other than Jesus, Napoleon, fat women or bowls of fruit. The Institute even rented out the old 69th Regiment Armory for maximum derivative impact. The streets around Lexington Avenue have been cleared. The mainstream press is covering the opening, so I'm wearing a nice pants suit, but with flats in case I need to run.

The cab drops me off a few blocks away, right into a calm but murmuring crowd. Mostly human cows: ladies who lunch. Eurotrash with fifty-mile-an-hour hairdos and white plasteeth slabs jammed into their gums. Hungry-looking culture vultures in threadbare cardigans and women with miniskirts so tight their buttocks look like canned hams wrapped in tarps. I push my way up Lex, poking asses with my shiv and occasionally throwing an elbow into the bridge of a nose or a bobbing patrician Adam's apple. I make it to the base of the steps just as a head cracks open on them and splatters my knees with blood.

She's black, nude, meaty, and still alive. A few belly rolls, thick brown nipples and half a face. The crowd cheers. I can't smell the blood over the cologne or the nasty underarm smell of the Euros on either side of me. I glance up and see another black woman tumbling down the steps. Her thighs bounce, but her arm cracks right away. She crumples only half-way down the stairs and screeches. A few hisses from the peanut gallery. I wink a few snapshots and run up the steps, shiv in my left hand, pepper spray in right.

"Lorraine Madison, *Art Round Table*," I say, punctuating my sentence with a knee to the balls of Vinshon Vins, who has another black woman ready to go, his fist in her nappy hair. She scampers off as I put the point of my shiv under the flesh of his chin. "Comment on race relations and the indentured subject, yes?"

Vinshon can't talk very well with his scrotum shoved into his pelvic bone but chokes out a "Yes . . . I want . . . you know, to decolonize the nude as text . . . interrogate the prurient gaze of . . . "

"Yeah yeah, volunteers?"

"What?"

"The women!" I have to get loud because the audience is picking their way over the bodies and blood-slicked steps behind me. The clicking of strappy heels is near-deafening.

"Nah, we own 'em. The Guggenheim bought me twenty for the show." Vins says. He frowns, and glances over my shoulder. "There goes my canvas." And people brush past my shoulders and make their way past the checkpoint to get into the exhibit proper. "What did you think?" he asks, like we're friends now.

I plan it perfectly. "Ham-fisted," I say and blink, taking a pic just as every trace of hope on Vins' face collapses into despair. "I couldn't think of a more obvious reference to *Nude Descending A Staircase Number Two* if I tried. Are we making art here, Vins, or just working out our white supremacist Midwestern angst? So you finally touched a black woman, I'm sure mom and dad back in Ypsilanti are scandalized." He opens his mouth to speak again, so I pump it full of mace and duck inside.

The exhibit proper is a bit overwhelming at first. The *smell* is anyway, combination slaughterhouse and that vague antiseptic smell of too much jism. A huge canvas predominates; it is tilted so Lauren Newman's intestines can slide down. Action painting, but too tentative as the life support equipment Newman is connected to is plainly visible on the scaffold above the work. Some strands of viscera twist gracefully enough down the canvas, but I'm not touched by the piece. Dissatisfied, I follow the screams to one of the side rooms.

Exhibit Room F is *Blue Feud.* A portly woman has volunteered. Her husband holds her coat, a mink in lavender, furs sliced thin and stitched to resemble corduroy. She squeals through a series of shots, long syringes puncture her arms and thighs. Excited and trembling, she can barely keep her skirt hiked up through the series. Her hips are bright white under the spotlight, the rest of the room is blacked out. Then a blast of fire from the corner (glimpses of men in the corners, lit by the flickering red moment) and the slugs hit her hard, like a boxer punching the heavy bag a hundred times a second. She falls and bleeds a rich azure. Her man stares on, not ready to weep yet. It's compelling. I video the blood, still blue and thick as ink, as it puddles near my shoes. Four assistants in military khakis, lightly dusted in flour, enter from the corners, grab her wrists and ankles and hoist her up and away.

"Her name was . . . " her husband begins, but a digitally deepened "No" from the corner interrupts him. "No name. No fame. No voice. She's a statistic now." Her husband sighs dramatically and rolls his eyes like a little girl, an odd juxtaposition to his salt-and-pepper hair and smartly knotted tie. He drops the coat onto the bloodied floor and stomps off, muttering into his lapel buttonphone for a lawyer.

Exhibit Room G is nearly another ruined moment. More volunteers. A hugely muscled black man is sodomizing from behind a young blonde just off the sorority corral. Bald of course, his pate is key lit through a light purple gel, to bring out the bronze in his skin. Americana hangs from the hastily constructed walls: a moose head, a rusted Route 66 sign, Ted Williams shilling Moxie Cola in orange and black tin. Muzak plays lightly in the background as the woman screams, "Oh god! God! My ass . . . it HURTS! Fuck me! Rape me! Fuck me you huge black motherfucking mandingo!" I bite the inside of my cheek, but the other onlookers aren't so forgiving. They laugh audibly. I smile. My eyes meet the would-be rapist's. He mouths the word silently between the huffs of sweaty fucking, "Man. DING. Go?" disgusted. I wink at him and we share a quick smile.

I'm followed out of that room, but the stalker doesn't know that I know. Much of the rest of the work elicits little more than a shrug. Phipps is in Exhibit Room K, skinning an indentured servant alive in a mock-up of a doctor's office, in too obvious a nod to George Grosz. *Beaten Child* would have been more interesting had the subject been a volunteer rather than a purchase, but most freeborn kids aren't sophisticated enough to offer up their lives for art's sake. Not enough guilt to exorcise. Back in the armory's grand hall, a dozen exhibition-goers at a time are locked into the gas chamber and killed. One makes a show of taking off his watch and throwing it to one of the artists before being shoved in. The great metal doors slam behind him, and the shower begins. The walls are thick though and so much else is going on that it is hard to make out the screams, or the futile second-thought fueled fists against the interior. I can only think *Good riddance,* and the chamber takes too long to shovel clean anyway. The crowd grows restless and disperses. My secret admirer walks off, following someone else.

I wander to an unobstrusive corner of the sculpture wing, nod to a heavily modified volunteer who now resembles Dasburg's lumpy *Lucifer* and take out my microrecorder. A lede comes to mind easily enough, but I see my stalker again. He's naked, revving a chainsaw over his head and coming straight at me. I manage to say "Banal but deadly!" drop the box, whip out my shiv again and duck his first pass. The little *poseur* is already breathing heavy. Too many cloves and too much crank, I bet. He whirls sloppily on his heel and turns to face me again.

"So, did I pan you a few months ago, or do you want me to make you famous now?" I ask him. He stands bowlegged, sweating. Black hair's all matted. He's meeting my eyes with that fake tough-guy stare. Me, I'm staring at his legs. His calves flex and spring. I duck and roll, then jab him in the thigh as the chainsaw chews the air over my head.

He yowls and that yowl becomes a typical artiste whine, "Art is dead! We herd our volunteers, or filthy lumpen chattel, into our deathwork! But where is the true freedom to explore?" He turns to the little crowd that gathered. "The critics have stolen it!" A few titters. I can hear them licking their lips. The crowd hungry for some spilled blood, blood that means something more than status or slavery.

They want the blood of someone who cares whether they lose it. That'd be a new thing to see at least.

Happy to oblige. I dart forward, ready to stab the little fucker right in the kidney. He spins around, swinging the chainsaw crazily. I fall back as he loses his grip on it. The saw whirls into the crowd, tearing through a few onlookers, its shrieking buzz crumbling into a strained rumble as the blade eats flesh and bone. Then the screams, *real* screams from pain unexpected and unpurchased, not the practiced affectations of the rich. Provocative!

The kid is faster than I thought. He's on me, sloppily avoiding the knee I put up to meet his balls. I turn him over and get into the mount position, ready to punch his teeth down his throat with the heel of my palm, but he has something. *Shit!* A Manolo Blahnik, heel-first and too fast, he gets my eye.

For a long moment I'm lost in the red haze of pain. He's not finishing me, but pontificating to the audience. I catch a snippet, some tortured babble about symbolic irony and putting out the eye of the critic. I can only think how heavy my face feels; the stump of the foot is still in the shoe. The world ripples in and out in throbbing waves, like a pleasant dream had under fiery sheets. *I'm pretty clever when I'm in agony,* I think, then I hear this distant tea-kettle whistle over the noise of the show. It's me screaming.

I breathe deep and remember my editor's training. Monet's *Water Lillies* is my trigger. It's a simple post-hypnotic suggestion. There is no horror, no pain, no fear. Only beauty. Only truth. Only the dance of light on water. Muted pinks and greens, a serene jumble of leaves. Put my pain away in the tiniest, darkest corner of my mind. *I am a critic. Critics stand above, always.* I pull the heel out of my eye and take to my feet.

They're all against me now. The women shuffle their feet under their gowns. One man's double chin bobs lustily. Fascination with gore is just so base.

I have a fifty-seven hundred dollar shoe in my hand, a cheek slick with eye jelly and an MA in Art History from a state university. They have three dozen well-toned, gym-trained limbs, a variety of weapons and jagged edges plucked from the other exhibits, a crazed and naked *poseur* goading them on.

It's hardly fair, really. "Jejune," I say, just over a whisper. To tantalize.

Murmur murmur, they murmur.

"Jejune!"

A collective gasp. I take a step forward.

"Trite."

The stalker's erection begins to wilt.

There is no pain. There is no fear. Only beauty. Only truth. I test the wall of flesh with another step forward. They step back as one. I take a picture of it with my good eye.

"An adolescent pandering to the tribal," I tell them, my face stern. Someone in the back titters nervously, like a hyena. But they're not even scavengers, these scum, they're herd beasts. Here's proof.

"BOURGEOIS!"

And the crowd breaks. My boy sinks to his knees. I don't even bother to plant the heel of the shoe into the base of his neck, a kindness I won't be offering again. I walk tall. The cows back up, squeeze tight to give me room to leave. Not one can meet my eye. I cross the length of the armory and walk down the steps. They're sticky with blood. Good thing I wore these cheap flats.

A slave on the corner is trying to hail a cab. I step in front of him and score one immediately.

Coda: It's been a week. Maiming is an occupational hazard, so my HMO hasn't come through. I'm public art now, in the lobby of St. Vincent's downtown. I have a bed, and treatment, but I have to hang the Manolo Blahnik from what's left of my eye socket during business hours to make good on the bill. Mostly it is only the children who stare, and the few provincials who got themselves a broken arm or a bullet wound while touring the big city, and both groups stare with kindness. I actually miss them at night, when the lobby empties out except for a single desk worker. Most of the lights are off after hours, but the Pelecanos installation *Tire Fire* is burning across the street on 7th Avenue's little traffic island. I like the way the reflections of flame and smoke play against the glass of the lobby's exterior wall.

Less interesting is the horrid bronze bust of some dead cardinal by the entrance. *A Portrait In Wrinkles* my intern named it when she came by to drop off some page proofs. *She* thinks she's clever, but I have to say she isn't far from wrong this time.

I think it's staring at me. After I file this month's column, I guarantee the hospital will melt the cardinal down.

It's An Honor To Be Nominated

"Congratulations!" read the subject heading of the e-mail. But no, I hadn't won a free cruise, or a much larger penis. My short novel, *Northern Gothic*, had made the final ballot for the Bram Stoker Award. The Stokers, managed by the Horror Writers Association, celebrate horror fiction, poetry, comics and "alternative media" by holding a banquet and giving out statuettes to the winners. It's just like the Oscars, except that nobody notices. This year the banquet was in New York, and I was invited. Invited to pay $65 for a weekend of panel discussions, pitch meetings to mass-market paperback publishers and dinner at the Helmsley Hotel on June 8th. What the hell, I thought, why not? I had no hope of winning, but there are seven words in English which are never untrue when said all together: "It's an honor just to be nominated."

Northern Gothic is dark fiction. It's a timeslip story: the racial hatreds of the Civil War Draft Riots drift over into modern day Chelsea and victimize a gay black wannabe dancer named Ahmadi. It was my poison pen letter to Manhattan and to all the people I've known who came to the city to make it big, sent the rents skyrocketing and infested the scene, only to run back to Ann Arbor or Columbus or Fresno once mama's money ran out. You know the type. They struggle along in publishing or the music industry for a few years and decorate their apartments with strings of chili pepper lights and mannequin torsos. They own (and sometimes actually wear) feather boas. And nearly all of them gained their romantic notions of Manhattan and life in it from dog-eared high school library books. *Northern Gothic* was supposed to be an antidote for that, my way of saying, "New York is full. Go home." But it was the horror and science fiction communities that picked up the book, not the hipsters. Fat guys in beards and *Buffy The Vampire Slayer* T-shirts, not those cute young women with bobs and Buddy Holly eyeglasses who never give me the time of day.

I wasn't the next Dennis Cooper after all. And if the sales reports are true, I'm not the next Stephen King either. I'm the first Nick Mamatas. So of course, I had to represent New York at the Stokers. I'm not really a hotel banquet sort of guy though. More of a Gray's Papaya sort (at least I was until those porkbelly-trading fatcats upped the price to 75 cents for a frank!) I didn't even own a suit. I found one a few days before the event, though, in Chinatown, fresh off the truck. There was still sweatshop sweat on the jacket. I borrowed a tie from my housemate, who did the dyke thing a few years ago and had plenty of semi-formal wear to spare. I passed on the shoes though, since I wasn't going to win. I was going to lose the Bram Stoker Award, and lose it really bad.

It became a joke and a PR thing. "Not only am I going to lose," I told my friends and even to two interviewers, "I'll come in fifth out of five. The only drama for me is whether I score the lowest vote total in Stoker history." I was about as confident as an Iraqi general, and for good reason. Within the horror community the Stokers are sometimes known as "the Strokers." Members of the HWA publicly vote on a preliminary ballot and then a final ballot. Since everyone knows who votes for what, logrolling is legendary. My own nomination sneaked in through the back door, thanks to the Additions Jury, whose job it is to make sure that deserving but obscure work gets noticed. *Northern Gothic* qualifies as obscure: it came out six weeks before the end of the year, from a publisher—Soft Skull Press—that never prints horror and rarely prints fiction, and I utterly failed to do gloryhole monitor duty at any of the many horror conventions held throughout the year. Clearly, I had no chance at all.

It gets worse. In the Long Fiction category I was up against the legendary fantasist Harlan Ellison, hot young writer Brian Keene (who was nominated in four categories!), popular Steve Rasnic Tem who won the category last year, and Nancy Echtemendy, whose story appeared in a widely read magazine. Plus, she's the treasurer of the Horror Writers Association. Would you buy new shoes to lose this badly? I wore my ratty old Doc Martens and my navy blue suit, to properly represent, Notorious B. I. G.-style.

I failed to represent, though. I was utterly anonymous. The woman running the registration desk gave me my badge and then said, "Want to buy a Stoker? The campaigning is horrible: 'Vote for me and I'll vote for you.' 'Vote for me and I'll put you in my anthology.' Nominees should hand out twenty dollar bills with 'For Your Consideration' written across the top."

"Wow, I'm nominated and I didn't do any of that!"

"Congratulations," she said, her smile not wavering for a moment, "and good luck."

Horror fiction has been in the sales doldrums for much of the past decade, and as such only a small community remains. There's an upside. The terror of the science fiction convention—the bearded know-it-all who smells of cat piss and denounces authors to their faces—has no Stoker banquet analog. Horror folks are normal, intelligent and friendly. The downside was that everyone seemed to know one another. Except me. I recognized a few names from bylines and the Internet, but the only conversations I managed to have were about how expensive the drinks were. The Helmsley charged $5.50 for a splash of ginger ale poured over a glass of ice. Even booze, the writer's friend, had abandoned me at seven bucks a bottle and two long lines, one for tickets, and then one for the bar to turn tickets into alcohol. It was like buying Russian toilet paper or something.

And "Good luck." Everyone who recognized my name from the final ballot wished me good luck. I made my ego-defense joke. "Oh, I'm doomed. Last place here I come!" And the same people who moments before were decrying the corruption of the Stroker Awards would just smile and say "Hey, you never know. Good luck." Of course, almost nobody I spoke to read the book—the few who did liked how I described the city. "Reminds me of why I'm staying in the hotel all weekend," one of them said.

Invisibility was an asset when it was time for the banquet. I had hidden my suit in the lobby bathroom and changed there. My tie, which my housemate had tied, had come undone. How un-punk rock! It took me a dozen tries to replicate the knot. I yanked all the tags I could see off the sleeves and saw that I was already fifteen minutes late. The dinner was underway!

Two other horror fans spotted me in the stall. They were in New York for the weekend and wanted to know if the lights were still on.

"Huh?"

"You know, for 9/11."

"Ah, yes, the Batsignals. No, those are gone. The hole is still available for viewing though."

"Is it by the hotel?"

"No, it's still where the World Trade Center used to be."

They didn't think I was funny. It was all too horrific, that someone might have to take the subway to see neatly swept-up carnage live, rather than on TV. Stick to the vampires, boys!

I hit the banquet hall fifteen minutes late, and slinked to a mostly empty table in the back of the room. I sat with more out-of-towners. They'd already been to Central Park and Grand Central Station and wanted to know what else they could do that was close to the Helmsley.

"Well, you can go back to Grand Central, go to the little Junior's they have in the basement and have a black and white cookie. That's New York."

"A black and white cookie! Yes, just like *Seinfeld!*"

I asked one guy if he was a writer. He was, and he had just had his pitch meeting. His book idea was confusing. A psychic detective who works for the cops and takes the form of the crime victims before the crime is committed but then he experiences the crime but can also stop it if it isn't supernatural. And that's just the first few pages.

I told him about *Northern Gothic*. He thought it sounded political. He asked if I was working on something else.

"Yes. H. P. Lovecraft's *On The Road,*" I said, describing a book idea I had come up with as a joke, but which is actually turning out to be quite writeable.

"Wow! One sentence," he said, excited. "Now that's a pitch."

A pause.

"They'd never take that in a million years though."

"Yeah, I know."

"Well, good luck. Maybe you'll win a Stoker tonight."

"Oh no, I'm doomed."

"Hey, you never know."

The appetizers came: prosciutto and fresh mozzarella with artichoke hearts, black olives and sun-dried tomatoes. I tried to distract myself by observing the Nazi efficiency of the servers, the long Stalinist lines of the cash bar (I sneaked a can of Coke in my jacket pocket. "Never again!" was my response to high-priced drinks) and the very odd choice of pork and cheese for an appetizer in a town with a fair number of Jews. But I couldn't. I was thinking about winning.

A Stoker Award of my very own. A stylized haunted house with my name on it. The little gray shack of success. Maybe it could happen. Harlan Ellison is a legend, but also a well-known asshole, and his lawsuit against online pirates had cost him some net-savvy fans. Brian Keene was nominated in four categories. Surely he wouldn't win them all? Maybe he'd lose mine. Ecthemendy's story was more magical realist than horror, and plus, as treasurer she may have made a few enemies within the HWA—because of infighting, not for anything she ever did. Tem's novella was strictly small press, and plus, he had his time last year. Clearly, the 'you never knows' had gotten to me. My New Yorker cool had melted into sweat—my own sweat—not cheap factory sweat, and my new suit was soaking in it.

I didn't have to wait long. I had barely eaten my appetizer, and those of the empty seats on either side of me, when salad was dumped into my plate. Then not four minutes later, my chicken marsala (this was a low budget banquet, *everyone* got the chicken), a twice-baked potato and some green beans came. I wondered what the vegetarian choice was. Probably more green beans and an extra dirty look from the food service Gestapo.

The cheesecake came and I saw why they snatched away the appetizers so quickly. The cheesecake tasted just like the stale mozarella of the first course! It must have been some bargain basement recycling deal. No way was this proper New York cheesecake. I wanted to get up and shout, "Don't eat the cheesecake! It's from out of town!" but instead I just turned to my tablemates and said, "Listen, when you go to the

Junior's annex in Grand Central, get some real cheesecake. I wouldn't feed this to a dead man's dog" (I don't normally talk like that, but I was in horror mode). They nodded. Then our coffees were snatched away.

Long story short. I lost. Tem won. My name was pronounced correctly though, which is always a happy surprise. And I got a certificate. It was embarrassing, though—I saw that all the other finalists were holding manila envelopes, but nobody had given me one. What's worse, being so anonymous that I had to remind the organization that nominated me that I had paid $65 for toejam cheesecake, or just getting a loser certificate in the first place? I got my envelope and was agog as I saw those immortal words of darkness inscribed upon it:

BETH ISRAEL MEDICAL CENTER
First Avenue at 16th Street,
New York, NY 10003.

Stealing office supplies. Now that's New York! And when I was leaving the hotel to retreat back across the Hudson to walk my dog, someone called my name. She was a cute redhead, with a short bob and a backless dress decorated with a cherry print.

"Nick?" she asked, smiling widely. Was it a fan? A real indie rockin' New York fan of *Northern Gothic?*

"You still have a clothing tag on your pants," she said. Then she ripped it off my ass.

June, 2002.

Impression Sunrise

I woke up and counted seven canvases, all finally complete. The aliens hadn't taken them. The aliens always get what they want. And they want pretty much everyone but me. I blew on the steam over my cup of coffee and then threw it at *Nude Ascending a Spaceship* (I had even left it by the window, but the hoity-toity bug-eyed monsters weren't interested).

It started only months ago. There was a flash of blinding light (The Beam, we call it now) and then the Louvre was empty. MOMA was ransacked by another silent orange flash, leaving nothing behind but nails, blank squares of bright white on the wall, and most of the Photography Department. The aliens are fickle in their taste. A four-year-old in Sweden had his finger-painting snatched the moment he completed it, but Whistler's *Nocturne in Black and Gold* is still on earth, though now buried deep underground and guarded by a battalion of useless Marines.

"Hey, that's business," my agent told me that afternoon at lunch. "Sometimes you're hot, sometimes you're not. We're still making money, we're getting a lot of good reviews." Rhonda was a five-foot tall bundle of energy wrapped in a bright pink business suit. Her makeup was troweled on (as usual) and she peered at me over the sunglasses she wore to hide her crows' feet (from men, not The Beam).

"I don't care about the goddamn galleries. Nobody is buying anyway. I can show wherever I want, because there isn't any competition anymore," I lied. I had plenty of competition, and they were all kicking my ass.

Rhonda frowned. "Dave, you know how it is." (Like most people with little to say, Rhonda liked to say the same things over and over. An advanced alien civilization, one capable of flinging itself across the galaxy, wouldn't come to Earth for water or gold or slaves. Their technology could handle all that. Only something uniquely human, something not found on their hyper-advanced world, could tempt them to come to Earth. And it wasn't.)

"Sex!" she shouted, loud enough to get my attention, and slammed her hand against the table. The entire café turned around. "I tell you, Dave, why couldn't it have been sex instead of art?" She stood up and flung her hands towards the sky (well, towards the painted tin roof of Café Reggio). "Take me! Take me, bend me over the Vietnam Memorial," (the aliens had taken that too, leaving the President to wonder what was wrong with all the nice statues of Lincoln and Washington he had), "and screw my brains out! Just leave Van Gogh alone! Warhol! Anyone!" People went back to concentrating on their coffee and pastry. These outbursts happened hourly in the Village, though it was usually me committing them, not my agent.

"Of course," Rhonda said, repeating what she had heard on tv, "the aliens wouldn't come here for sex any more than you would fly to Africa to stick your dick into a warthog or wildebeest, but still, they seem to have some kind of aesthetic sense."

I drifted off again, into the memories of my career.

#

For the first few weeks, my friends and I had worried. Phipps had called me up to his loft (well, his garret with a window) to tell me something. "I know how to save our work for the human race," he whispered to me, while glancing out the window, watching for The Beam. "Look." With a dramatic little flick of his wrist, he yanked a dirty tablecloth off his milk-crate-and-chicken-wire pedestal and unveiled a sculpture. Abstract, just finished and gleaming. It was okay. It curved in on itself, like a crazy eight trying to leap off the pedestal. At least it wasn't an alien head, a spaceship or a raised middle finger in plaster, like most of Phipps' stuff had been since the aliens ripped off his entire show. They had taken that stuff too.

I turned to Phipps and shrugged. He smiled. "Look," he said, and covered one of the curves of the sculpture with his thick fingers. "Envision this sculpture without this line." I did, and it definitely would have improved the sculpture had that bit not been there. "You see. Damage your work. Make it unacceptable. But don't forget. Never forget." He tapped his temple and smiled at me, showing off his yellow ratbastard teeth (cloves, we all smoked them). "Never forget what you dream of. Art is in the mind."

"So I do something wrong, and tell people just to ignore what I put in?"

"Yes, exactly." We smiled and high-fived one another and spent the rest of the night drinking gin from Phipps' flask (he hanged himself a week later).

I had been in the middle of a dry spell, but Phipps inspired me that day. I went home, dusted off a canvas I was keeping under my bed (it was too terrible to look at, I thought, and I couldn't finish it with the aliens watching me) and worked on the piece all night. It was abstract, and busy, about my stomach condition and my latest breakup and about just feeling trapped in my skull. I finished it, and added a yellow stripe diagonally across the whole piece, to ruin it.

I woke up at noon (hating myself) and spent five more hours cleaning off every bit of yellow from the piece. I even got my lenses and scraped out bits of dried yellow (they were no more than a single horsehair thick) from the cracks in the canvas. The aliens didn't take it (oh how I waited for The Beam). They hadn't taken anything of mine, nothing at all. All my friends' work was being spirited away. All the paintings I had admired were gone. My stuff was stuck on this planet, along with every velvet Elvis and a busload of blood-and-chocolate-drenched performance artists. They hated me. They loved everything (we thought —maybe they were taking everything up there to shred, or eat, I sometimes reminded myself) Earth had. Everything but me. I sucked. "You don't suck," Rhonda said, "You're getting two pages in *Artpapers* in June."

"Alan?" (Jacobson, a friendly critic and good lay).

"No." Rhonda's face deflated like all her plastic surgery just gave out.

"Hmm?"

"Alan's dead."

"Shit." (I didn't have to ask. Some art critics had taken to blasting the aliens in print, claiming that their confiscations demonstrated a pedestrian taste. Most of these critics ended up being greeted by The Beam, which removed their intestines from their bodies, usually right as the articles went to press).

"Not Alan. Linda Poulos. We want you to do a painting. Two weeks."

"I hate doing paintings, Rhonda. The Beam never comes. The Beam won't be coming for me." My skin tingled under my sweater from the heat. Painting was one thing, doing a goddamn painting was another. Doing a painting meant being a trained ape for The Beam, or for the culture vultures who loved it. Doing a painting meant spending weeks on a piece, and then inviting every yuppie grazer and venture capitalist in town to watch you clean it up, make a few marks with the knife, and put the finish on it. Then (according to theory) The Beam would come and take the painting away, and the crowd would applaud (like they had just sat through Cats or something). "I don't do paintings."

"You'll do this one, okay?" Rhonda said. "You know, I found you when you had just gotten off the bus from Wheeling. I knew you when." (She was repeating herself again. She knew me when I was sketching the tall ships down at the Fulton Street Seaport, back when I would go home with anything in a muscle shirt for a free meal and a night on a mattress, back when I was a week from hustling on the streets and don't you know, you dance with who brung yuh, and goddamn it, she had brung me and I was going to waltz my cute little nuts off).

"Fine. Just could you, you know, shut the hell up for the rest of lunch? I've got a headache."

Rhonda smiled. "Try declaring it art. Maybe The Beam will take it away, the aliens will all get headaches and leave us alone." I had to grin at that. Three days into the crisis, the President had Christo wrap a warhead in pink cellophane, to tempt the aliens. They took it up to their ship(s), but even that didn't stop The Beam (the aliens also took Mr. President's Jack Daniels belt buckle, apparently in a fit of pique).

I couldn't paint for the rest of the day. I walked around the neighborhood. Most of the galleries were boarded up, or had been rented out to art forgers (The Beam never took a copy, which is how the world found out that Michelangelo's David was fake), or back to warehouse firms. The streets seemed wider now that there were no street artists hawking their crap to people. There was only me.

I did some sketches. I read the paper. Schnabel had killed himself too (drank a quart of paint), the day before yesterday. Parsons School of Design announced that it was shutting down its Fine Arts division, because the freshmen just kept painting aliens and spaceships and screaming college students being sucked out of dorm room windows. The commercial art department was still going strong, though, the article said. (I think I spotted a shoe store ad with a line drawing by Chuck Close on the opposite page.) I decided to puke up the cannoli I had for lunch and take a nap.

Rhonda called me twelve times a day. She would never come out and ask how it was going (she would instead ask "Are you busy?" and hope the answer was yes) but the pressure was on. I spent whole days on the computer, looking at scans of the stuff the aliens had taken. I missed Monet most of all (even though I couldn't stand him back when I was in school). I checked my email compulsively (every ten seconds, I think). My sister wrote me:

From: artchica82@hotmail.com
To: chemicalking@lsh.org
RE: YEEESSSSS!!!!!!!!!!!!

Fina-fucking-ly! Davey, The Beam grabbed one of my prints! I had just finished it, and blew some of the graphite off my signature, and they took it away! It rocked. The beam was like staring into the sun, like dancing with static electricity. And you never liked my shit, nobody ever did. HA! I knew I was ahead of my time. I guess you have to be an alien to understand my work. :o).
Luv,
Stacey.

Stacey was seventeen-years-old and a moron. But The Beam had blessed her. She still lived in Wheeling, for God's sake. That night my bed sheet was tight around my neck, but I couldn't keep from kicking. The plaster around the eyehook I drilled into the ceiling gave way. I hit the floor hard (and twisted my ankle) but that was all.

The work went slowly. I sat on my windowsill and threw paint tube caps at the pigeons. I didn't change my underwear or brush my hair (or look in the mirror). I shaved blind, cutting myself too many times to care about. At night I clutched my pillow and screamed, "Why doesn't anybody love me!" at the light bulb in the bare fixture over my bed.

I would turn to the window, hoping to see The Beam descend, bright-streaking-yellow across the blue-black night, and spirit something away. I never caught it, but I knew the aliens were still collecting pieces. When I'd go out in the morning for coffee, my old friends would be all smiles. They were happy, they laughed with one another over the theft of their work. Poseurs. Bastards. I was ignored, like a ghost, or litter, or the sounds of traffic. I started calling in for coffee in the mornings again (the Mexican who would trot up six flights of steps with a sopping paper brown bag every day didn't care for art. It was his pleasure to serve me. Even the coffee cup said so).

Six days later, I thought I had something. It would be representational (the aliens preferred pictures they could easily identify, scuttlebutt said), and I would sketch and then paint it on the spot. Rhonda and the other bastards would just have to sit up all night with me while I worked, instead of popping in to ooh and aah at The Beam. I filled my notebook with sketches, though. I wasn't going to be doing any spaceships, but something celestial. Maybe a crescent moon; the idea of absence was important (a little ham-fisted maybe, but think of my audience). A crescent moon over a half-empty city. Half-empty because someone had sold off all the beauty to the highest bidder. A lot of black, a lot of work with the knife, to keep the party happy. Then, at about three in the morning, I would start painting in little dabs of light, one for each office window dotting the shadowed cityscape. I hoped Rhonda wouldn't start counting each one (under her breath), but she was probably gauche enough to do exactly that (with enough champagne in her). I practiced air kissing in front of the mirror, brushed my teeth and went to bed.

The maid (hired by Rhonda) came by the next day to do the dishes (they had piled up in the tub), and swept out the place. The caterers came by with three loaves of bread, two bunches of grapes, three kinds of cheese, a case of wine, a case of champagne and a case of the hard stuff (priorities). Rhonda showed up just after dusk.

"Put the easel by the window," she said, brightly.

"Why?"

She just frowned at me and went to answer the doorbell.

It was dark by the time everyone had shown up. Linda Poulos took my hand with both of hers and pumped my arms like she was trying to jack up a van. I air kissed the other women and a few of the men. They were a slightly older crowd, all in ties or business skirts and sneakers (nobody who has to get to my six-story walkup wears heels). One guy even had a headset on, and did a few trades while in the john. (Get me twenty-five shares of Cisco—flush!) What was he even here for? My mouth was drier than ten glasses of White Zinfandel. We drank for a few hours, and I did my best to hold off the time with round after round of drinks, and slice after thin slice of cheese. It was midnight when Rhonda's eyes narrowed at me. By twelve-thirty her jaw had locked shut. She marched up to me and sang "Get. On. With. Iiit!" into my ear, as cheerful as Dachau.

Everyone took their seats, and I moved to the easel. I took the tarp off the canvas and said (over my shoulder) "Hope everyone has already used the facilities, it is going to be a long night." I crossed my arms and smiled at the blank canvas, and squinted to see the grain of the sheet. My pencil was tucked behind my ear. Someone poured a drink. A cell phone rang, but was quickly clicked off (thank God). Rhonda cleared her throat meaningfully (it meant "I'm going to kill you, Dave, if you don't get on with it").

I took the pencil from my ear and put it to the canvas.

I took it away, turned to the small audience, snapped the pencil in half and let both pieces fall out of my hands to the floor.

The Beam washed over my eyes like a wave of translucent orange juice. Every pore was alive, every hair on my body decided to pull away (and in opposite directions, too). Through the haze I could see Rhonda drop her glass and ten pairs of hands slap together like seals' flippers. I couldn't hear the applause, though, not through the low grind of The Beam (like ten million cinder blocks being dragged across asphalt). I let go and my bladder gave way. I think Linda smiled.

Then there was nothing but the sound of a curtain flapping and a smoggy breeze. When I woke up, my vision still swam in an orange light, like I was inside the sun looking out. Linda's hair was perfect. The crooked front teeth of the Cisco guy were perfect. The symmetry of the lines on Rhonda's face was astonishing. I cried in her lap.

"They like blank canvas pieces," she whispered to me. Her lips smiled against my ear.

Things are looking better now. The world is bathed in light, like an impression at sunrise, like a painting I used to admire.

Why I Flame

Bloody Q-Tips and anonymous cyberbombs: professional flamer Nick Mamatas

(from the *Village Voice*)

I am a sick man. I am a spiteful man. I am an unattractive man.

For a living.

Eleven years ago, in college, I discovered the Internet on a dumb terminal. Within five minutes, I managed to get myself "killed" in a multiuser game. I don't remember what I did to deserve death, but I did it extremely well.

I spent the next decade soaked in flames and have made a career out of it.

As companies try to build their brands through newsgroups, e-mail feedback, and Web forums, the job title "Professional Flamer" stands ready to be penciled into the office hierarchy, right under "Chief Yahoo" and just over "Minister of Indie Culture." In service to our employers, we flamers slither across the Internet—a realm where rudeness is a form of currency—and take out the customers, competitors, and wannabes who target businesses out of misplaced rage or the need to feel important.

White-shirted execs don't want to dirty their hands with the kinds of ugly, eviscerating messages we plant. PR flacks still don't know how to deal with online haters, much less which ones to take seriously. Flamers know. We emerge informally from marketing departments, help desks, the ranks of committed freelancers and system administrators. When an attacker needs to be smacked down, we volunteer. After a while, our talent for spewing vitriol gets noticed, encouraged, and exploited, sometimes even becoming an official part of our jobs. We don't often get paid for the extra work, except in the sheer joy we feel for a job well done. We, too, have misplaced rage and the need to feel important, but we have corporations backing our missives, the way a terrorist driving a truck bomb through a crowded thoroughfare has God on his side.

Sander Hicks, the publisher of Soft Skull Press, once asked me to flame a minor figure in the rock pantheon. The artist was angry because his unsolicited manuscript hadn't been met with the solicitude he felt he deserved, so he flamed first, calling Soft Skull "fucked up," "phony," and "disrespectful." "The godfather of punk is out to kill me now," Hicks wrote to me. "Could we please either write him a formal rejection letter or just flame him?"

We could. Officially acting as a senior editor, I flamed him over e-mail and bounced his manuscript. He never wrote back. It's not always that easy.

Dostoyevsky ranted about flames way back in 1864, in *Notes From the Underground.* "When petitioners used to come for information to the table at which I sat, I used to grind my teeth at them, and felt intense enjoyment when I succeeded in making anybody unhappy," he wrote. I wish I felt that good. Instead, flames eat away at me.

A meeting with friends ends early because I know there is e-mail waiting for me: someone out there needing to be crushed. Dinner with my girlfriend is interrupted because someone flamed one of my online columns and hasn't yet been soundly refuted. When writing, I chew on my fingers until they bleed, then spend the next morning cleaning my keyboard with a Q-tip. Somewhere along the line, this compulsion became a job. Now I can respect myself, just not in the mornings.

I write columns for two popular underground Web sites—Disinformation (**www.disinfo.com**) and the *Greenwich Village Gazette* (**www.nycny.com**). Feedback from my readers is nasty, brutish, and short, but I've begun to seek it out. My positive review of violent anti-Nazi organizations provoked a windfall; an army of liberals denounced me for being worse than a Nazi for applauding attacks on Nazis. I fired back: "If beating up a Nazi makes one worse than a Nazi, then what does that make the Warsaw ghetto fighters, who actually shot some Nazis? You do realize that your logic leads right to the crematorium and the mass grave, don't you?"

With every flame , my employers rack up the Web hits, as my articles are referred to time and again by the very people who insist my work be stricken from the Net. Will I call my opponents shit-flinging bonobos, threaten lawsuits, accuse them of illiteracy, or insist that I am much better looking than that old has-been Deborah Harry, as long as the conversation keeps going? Of course I will, and I will get a few more hits every time.

Flames are even becoming a standard part of public relations. Chris Owens, late of Creative Labs's marketing, ran the news servers for the company. The newsgroups superficially resembled Usenet newsgroups, but with one crucial difference: instead of being in the public domain, these groups were owned and operated by the company, for the company's benefit. Owens stoically withstood the flames from customers who couldn't get their Soundblasters to work. When Creative's production schedule clashed with reality, Owens, a technical marketing engineer, was the public face of the firm. When someone wouldn't read the manual, Owens had to go over basic instructions step-by-step. And he wasn't allowed to retaliate. Months after he left the job, I ask him if he ever flamed the clientele. "No," he says, "and when I did, I did it subtly."

In the wilds of Usenet, corporate flaming exists, even though the corporations attached to the newsgroup don't control the venue. The corporate heads of White Wolf Publishing, which makes role-playing games, can't banish their testy fans, but employees and freelancers can wage flame wars and protect the corporate image. After several people complained about a recent rewrite of a game, longtime White Wolf writer Deird'Re M. Brooks singled out a customer and flamed him on **alt.games.whitewolf**. She mocked the guy, saying he'd made it his "life's mission to tell us all how evil" the new rules and story line were. Brooks dismissed his complaints as "egotistical" and "worthless." She tried to make the fan sound hysterical, saying he wanted the game's latest edition "EXPUNGED FROM THE EARTH." Brooks, who didn't return voice e-mails, wasn't speaking as a corporate representative, but she was clearly expressing a sentiment shared by her superiors.

Public relations used to mean dealing with a distant consumer base as a mass. Now it means dealing with individuals, some of whom will be downright vicious. Recitations of press releases won't do it anymore. Corporations are very protective of their public images, and many have already unleashed their watchdogs to prowl the Web, looking for anticorporate flames to snuff out. Professional flamers will only become more common. We were here before you were, when ".edu" and ".gov" anchored most e-mail addresses, and when the Web was but a dream.

You're going to need us socially crippled flamers. We'll spread like brush fires. As Dostoyevsky might say today, we are developing a taste for it. Soon we shall contrive to be born somehow from an idea, an idea that needs to be beaten into the heads of every one of you. But enough; I don't want to write more from the underground.

September 2000.

Joey Ramone Saves the World

It was a day later, five am Monday, and you were riding down the Long Island Expressway, half-high from diesel fumes and the rumbling of marbles in the engine of your father's sardine-tight Volkswagen Rabbit. The tinny warble of the traffic reporter collapsed into the happy beat of "I Wanna Be Sedated." The female announcer, a bit too happy to be reading the news, explained: "Punk rocker Joey Ramone is dead." You gasped, the first sound you'd made since shuffling into the car an hour before. It was cold for April.

She went on, her sentences poorly punctuated by AM static and crackle. The Ramones started punk. He was born in 1952. His name was Jeffrey Hyman. Bruce Springsteen was a fan and Joey wrote "Hungry Heart" for him. *No, that's wrong,* you thought. *Springsteen wrote it for Joey, but then kept it for himself.* You grumbled audibly.

"What's wrong?" your father said, half-singing, half-gruff.

"He was the same age as Mom."

"What?"

"Joey Ramone was one of my favourites. He was a singer in a punk band." Then, "Sshhhhh," because you wanted to hear the rest of the obituary, and because talking made you gulp down fumes and want to puke. It was still twenty-five minutes till Jersey City. For a moment you forgot you threw your shrew of a girlfriend out of the house three days before, on Good Friday even, because she wouldn't stop dancing around in her panties while you answered an e-mail, the subject of which you couldn't remember any more anyway. You only remembered Joey, and the fact that he saved your world.

#

Or.

#

Jeff was a tall man. From your perch you were able to keep track of his head, or at least his unkempt rat's nest of black hair, for a long while. He was the last of the comrades standing. You did your best to help, kicking a Beaux-Arts bunch of limestone grapes off a cornice and onto a brace of Blue Shirts, and even whipping it out and pissing on the crowd below, but a Libre trios finally cornered Jeff. One, in red and gold, somersaulted off the corner of a rubbish bin and brought him to the ground, then his spangled and sequined partners ran in, grabbed Jeff's legs, and started twisting and cracking. You could almost hear bone crunch under their boots and truncheons. It sounded like the dog back at the squat chewing on a chicken back. Jeff's blood stained their hands and leotards and even their garish sequined masks. But the revolution would win, you knew. Jeff Hyman saved the world.

#

Or.

#

"Whiskey," you said, holding up a shot glass in your right hand. "Gun," you said, hoisting your pistol. It was Thursday night. Revival night. What else would you be doing? "Whiskey," you said with the rest of the room, praising the Lord. "Gun," you said, your voice resonant and deep like His. You were proud of that. And then the Dee Dee rose, signalling the next act of the liturgy.

"Gabba gabba hey hey / came from heaven," you chanted, and you were hugged by the woman next to you. She smelled of sweat and baby powder. Somewhat like the President when you hugged her last week. There was nothing to fear. Next Thursday you'd be in China with your whiskey and your gun, getting hugs from your brothers and sisters on the other side of the planet. You were one of them. They were one of you. Like the Holy Quartet. And everyone believed. You're all kids of the kingdom now. Joey Ramone had saved the world.

#

"August, 1974," Douglas said. He yawned, to wind himself up. His fish belly poked out from under his T-shirt. "I was so fucking there! I knew it, even fucking then. I was eighteen-fucking-years-old and I pissed myself over a man. Joey was so tall. He was fucking wasted. Fucking wasted." An aside, cleverly rehearsed, to himself: "Man, I am so fucking wasted. I am so fucking wasted. If I repeat myself, you know I am fucking wasted."

He waved his hands about like he wanted to hug CBGBs. "Wasn't like this then. Nineteen fucking seventy-four. Who here was even born then?" Doug demanded. He licked his lips. Three girls were listening to him, or at least looking at his stupid salt-and-pepper sideburns. One of them, Melba, bi-racial, kohl-eyed and sniffling from the feather boa around her neck, was born then. She was two, even. In Connecticut. Now she was in the club she had read about as a kid. She even owned the T-shirt. Melba knew better than to wear it to the club. She wore her Ramones shirt, but one from the *Animal Boy* era when Richie was in the band. She thought that must make her suck somehow. She was frowning about *something*, anyway. Douglas probably thought so too, but you found a way to forgive her.

"This is fucking shit," Douglas said. "This shit is laminated for your protection. There weren't even any fucking lights on back then. Just Joey, holding onto the mike stand like it was his mother's fucking tit. Holding on for dear life! And singing. 'One-two-three-four!'" Douglas pumped his fist in the air and shouted, loud enough to make the barback turn around and roll her eyes, "One-two-three-four!" His arm was meaty—like he lifted—and tattooed. Old school. Green bullshit skulls and thorns.

You knew that was bullshit. You knew not to say anything, because Douglas was "so wasted" as he said yet again. Later you told Melba that it was bullshit, that Douglas wasn't there that day because only one person who didn't work at CBs was there and it was a girl, and because Tommy sang at the first gig. Joey was on drums. You read that in *Creem* last year. Melba rolled her eyes, but kissed you anyway, and groped you up against the scooped-out stucco walls of CBGBs. You wished you were in a band. Then you'd have a sticker or a tape to give her. But the kiss was good, like you hoped it would be. She tasted of Red Stripe and Chiclets. Tomorrow was back to high school for you.

#

The invasion was a slow one. Juan Morais was barely known to the public before his troops were on the border. You watched the Sunday afternoon news shows, you read the *Times*, so you knew it was coming. You didn't know the President would fold, and would throw open the borders to let them in. Jeff did know, though, and told you the first time you met him.

"Oh, please, that's a conspiracy theory," you said. You were in line for gas for dad, a pillowcase full of bills in one hand's sweaty grip, a five-gallon can behind you. Wednesday was diesel day. Jeff was hard to believe. He was sniffing a rag, after all.

"Happens all the time, dude," he said between sniffs. "The economy goes to hell, and fascism seems like a good idea to big business. Morais was elected in Brazil! Fucking elected. The Mexicans just surrendered. This ain't like Double-you Double-you Two. Back then building a Navy could end the Depression. But not with gas costing fifteen thousand bucks a gallon."

Make that seventeen thousand bucks a gallon. The greasy monkey hobbled out and flipped the numbers on the sign over the pumps to a chorus of deep-throated boos. Jeff huffed loudly, like he was sneezing into the fucking rag or something. The gas station attendant backed away from the crowd. He undid his jumpsuit a bit, to show that he was carrying. Everyone shut up then, except for Jeff.

"Somebody once said that, when fascism came to America, it would look like patriotism, but I think people are too pissed off for that. They're going to march over us." Another long huff into the rag, one so hard it felt like it was your face was the one going numb. Heat carried the fumes across the tightly packed queue. "But we can stop 'em."

#

You learned the Prophet's False Dilemma as a child. You knew "whiskey" and "gun" before you even learned that you were one of Us. It was a century before you were born and two after The Ramone had died when Old Douglas was faced with his fatal choice. He was an old man, nearly eighty, and living on the Lower East Side, close to what you now knew as the Holy Bee. And Old Douglas woke up every morning for no reason, for he had nothing to do, and turned to his end-table. On it was a shot glass, empty except for a ring of sticky old booze, and a bottle of whiskey. Also, a revolver.

And each day he'd wake up, slowly pull one eyelid free of evening eyescum and think.

Whiskey? he'd think. *Or gun*. Sometimes it took as long as five hours to decide. Usually it was the sun crossing the sky to its noon apex that kept him alive. The rays of the sun would come through the window and hit the bottle at just the spot to make the booze sparkle, to make the centre of the liquid shimmer like syrupy gold.

But Morning One was an overcast day. Old Douglas had that snub-nosed revolver pushed hard against his temple, so hard that he might not have even been interested in the bullets penetrating his skull. He wanted the barrel to do it. And then Douglas was slain, not in the flesh, but in the spirit. He jerked wildly and was thrown back down upon his mattress. The shot glass wobbled against the tabletop, a little *wuddlawuddla* that became the Call of the Ramone: "Gabba gabba. Gabba gabba."

And then He was there, skin white as bone, hair black as night, voice deeper than the oceans, eyes flat and grey like slate. And He spoke to Old Douglas—now the Prophet—and the Prophet transcribed the Word of Joey on some conveniently located cocktail napkins. He gathered about

Him a trio of followers to play guitar, bass and drums, instruments not played live since the Intellectual Property and Creativity Protection Act of 2030, which had banned live instrumentation lest some wayward strumming unwittingly plagiarized an existing chord progression. The True Prophets took to the streets and to the clubs, gathered about them a devoted cult of fans and co-religionists and were eventually gunned down on the streets.

But a century later the God of Abraham was dead and you and he and that guy over there and ol' whatsername were all One Of Us. The nation-state had collapsed in a spasm of three-chord brotherhood. The aesthetics of Ramonism were full of options thumping backbeat upon which nearly anything could be built without rancour, censorship, or vicious iconoclasm. After the final 'gabba hey' of the evening, the gun was flushed down the ritual toilet and the whiskey flowed like sweat in a mosh pit. Some boy was licking it off your belly when you fell to the ground and began speaking in tongues.

#

College was easier than high school. All you had to do was wear the shirt, the one you stole from your uncle. The one that still smelled like pot a hundred washings after you'd stolen it from the drawer of stuff he couldn't wear since getting his job at the insurance company. The Ramones, from the ancient All the Way tour, 1981. Marky on the drums, and his name joining the others around the white-eagle seal, and the rest of the shirt was black, thank God. The kids with the white shirts and black seals had obviously been brainwashed by their parents, who equated wearing black with worshipping the Devil. The black shirt was entré to the tribe.

A nod in a lecture hall. A well practiced, lopsided smile while walking along the quad. A seat at a table in a campus cafeteria. "Hey," you'd say, or he would.

"Hey," you'd say back, and often say nothing else, until someone turned on the radio and played Debbie Gibson or Erasure. Then you'd snort, and the other members of the tribe would smile.

The banner on the wall over your bed helped too. Not Melba but another girl, a white one named Jennifer, as they nearly all seemed to be named those days, lingered by the doorway till your roommate invited her in, but she was interested in talking to you, in dicking around with your CDs. She played with your tie-fighter model. You made love that night to most of *End of the Century*, or at least to the last half of "High Risk Insurance." You jabbed her in the eye with your elbow in the middle of "Danny Says," but it was a slow song so you were able to apologize and be generally soothing. You lost your erection during "The Return of Jackie and Judy," and she gagged on your penis for most of "This Ain't Havana." You giggled at that, stupidly and in time with the "Na na / na na na" of the tune. That made her stop and laugh too. But before the CD ended and went on to repeat your back and belly were soaked with sweat, and her nails tickled your sides.

Now that you think back to it, maybe her name was Jessica.

End of the Century is actually a pretty underrated album.

#

You read Jeff's pamphlet one day after morning exercises down at the plant. The photocopy was fresh and smudged your hands with its ink, but you got the gist. Working-class revolution, fight the "Libre" faction at the point of production. Yadda yadda, easier said than done, right? Right. The union was gone, the shop steward fired, pay had been cut again and there was mandatory calisthenics in the parking lot every morning. Management even dusted off the old *Domino's Sugar Employee Songbook*. "An Ode to the Cane (Sugar, That Is)" was just about your least favourite song ever.

But the pamphlet had something interesting to say: "Revolution—Mafia Style." You don't need to convince everyone to join the revolution, just one special person in the right place, at the right time, ready to monkeywrench. Find a few friends. Do something.

You ate lunch out by the water that day, to watch the military patrol boats criss-cross the East River. Usually you couldn't stomach it out there, especially since the projects of the Lower East Side had been turned into concentration camps. The breeze smelt like badly burnt beef all the time now.

"Good thing the bosses still like their sugar, eh?" he said. You knew the voice, deep but melodic. Every sentence was a song. Jeff and a few of the guys from the plant were on the lip of the pier, dangling their feet over the river and eating sandwiches. Jeff was wearing a wetsuit and sitting in a puddle. He must have swum the river for the meeting. You skootched closer. Douglas, a guy whose neck was about as thick as your thigh and three times as veiny, shot you a withering look, but Jeff just smiled.

"That kid's a friend of mine. Let him in. I'll vouch."

"You're the boss," Douglas said.

"No, dude, we're all the boss, or none of us."

That night Douglas hummed and scatted to himself (God, he was annoying) as you helped him spike fifty tons of granulated sugar with some chemical Jeff had come up with. Tomorrow it would all be in little white packets. Only *los ricos* could still afford morning coffee anyway.

#

And, in a flash, it was revealed. A being, monstrous and beautiful. Cosmic jelly, almost, golden and filling the holes in the inky black sky. You couldn't understand the physics of it all, no more than a dot on a piece of paper would be able to figure out, from its 2-D perspective, what the fingers reaching for it might be. God is infinite and indeed in the details, but nowhere else. God is whiskey, constantly pouring over the rocks of the material world.

You could taste It. It was in you suddenly, hammering away at the specks of chemicals and consciousness that kept you hemmed into a mere I. You expanded, engulfing the planet, and rose ever higher and deeper. Finally, you were huge, with your heart and muscles and bones and brain a flat sheet stretched over the curve of spacetime, and the rest of the universe minding its own business inside you. You turned your perception within, because the face of the space beyond that of the twenty-billion-light-year plane you were covering like a military bedsheet was too horrible to bear.

And You looked within, into the bowels of Yourself and saw Earth. Not one, but billions, little more than *E. coli* peppering the membrane of your colon. And then You knew how right You were. All those Earths were one of You. You had saved them all.

#

A 3.0 would have bagged you two months in Europe and all the fancy-ass crap you could fit in a backpack. You got a 2.8. Grandma promised you'd get a plane ticket anyway, but you'd be back in a week and had better start looking for a job the second you landed back at LaGuardia.

"Two point eight. Jesus Christ, what were you goddam doing in school? Go, go on your trip, then come back ready to be a man. Two point five, grandma would have bought you a one-way ticket!"

You picked Brazil. Pop assumed it was for the tits. Grandma wondered why you didn't want Italy, to see your cousins. Brazil it was, though. São Paulo, which was Italian enough anyway. And in Brazil, The Ramones packed stadiums.

You don't remember the flight. You barely even remember sleeping atop your luggage in the hothouse airport terminal while customs agents and swarthy midget cops pulled apart everyone's bags. The water was hot coming out of the tap in your one-room pension. You were directed to a concrete pillbox with a hole on the floor for you to shit and piss in (Grandma spared pretty much every expense) but didn't care. You'd pee on the streets like the kids did, the kids with those telltale black T-shirts and surly faces. The fans were coming to see them, appearing on corners and near bars like late-night crows looking for early corn. Three days.

Finally, you didn't mind the heat. Sweat shook itself off you, thanks to the roar. The roar you felt before you heard, a mile away from the stadium. The locals, mostly dark or at least olive, fell away as you walked up the cobblestoned streets, and your people replaced them. The fans marched towards it, a bowl of light under the blue-black sky. And that hollow joyous roar became distinct.

"Ah ah ah, Ra-mone-es."

"Ah ah ah, Ra-mone-es."

"AH AH AH."

"RAH."

"MON."

"ES."

You sang the old soccer chant too, instantly adopting the three-syllable version of the name like everyone else did. The local kids. The pasty and potato-faced German tourists. The other Americans. "Ra-mon-es! Ra-mon-es!" You shouted it in the face of the hard case who checked your ticket, and he didn't even blink. He was probably deaf from being so close to ground zero all day. For another hour you heard nothing more than "Ah ah ah! Ra-mone-es!" and occasional cheers for a roadie or a lighting technician or for a beach ball gone wild bouncing across the crowd.

Then ONE-TWO-THREE-FOUR and the world was torn a new asshole by fifty thousand people screaming. Joey grasped the mike stand and leaned on it hard. It was the only thing keeping him from being blown off the stage, through the seats and parking lots, and out into the sea. Johnny and Dee Dee squatted like sumo wrestlers and cradled their instruments. "Blitzkrieg Bop" was over before your brain had even figured out that your ears had heard it. ONE-TWO-THREE-FOUR, then a song. "ONE-TWO-THREE- FOUR," Joey would cry, or Dee Dee would, then another song. No ballads. No slow tunes. No bullshit repartee. Joey didn't even say, "SÃO PAULO ROCKS!"

Everyone already knew.

It was dawn by the time they were done, or maybe Joey and the boys had just shattered the black lacquered dome of night and the sun was out by default, never to set again.

You didn't even realize that one of the guys you stepped over as you staggered out of the arena was a half-crushed corpse. A street kid, obviously, in a relief-worker-provided T-shirt and mismatched shoes. He had probably died with that gas-soaked hanky over his face. He had to dull the pain of broken bones somehow.

#

Juan Morais didn't so much escape the shantytowns of Brazil as he picked them up on his shoulders and took them with him all the way to the top. He never even officially joined the Brazilian army; instead he just killed a soldier and took his place. He knew enough about the local drug lords and Communists to make it worth his commander's while to keep him around. He crawled his way up the chain of command on a ladder of corpses.

The coup was easy enough, when the time came. He spoke to the people in the language of the streets, in the terms of Mexican *lucha libre* and Portuguese soap operas. There was good and evil in the world, and by God and Virgin he was going to stop evil in the name of good. He wasn't complacent to fan himself in the presidential palace either. Morais did a road tour, filling up stadiums and arenas, sometimes at gunpoint, but often just through force of personality. Brazil was his. He even rearranged regional borders in an attempt to capture his profile in maps.

When Morais moved north, it didn't take a single bullet to march across Central America. Venezuela had turned off the oil spigot at his request and the Middle East had been turned into a glass parking lot a few years previously, so the US was weak and pink, like a fat baby. Morais wanted in. A few hawks in the Air Force wanted to bomb him back to the shit from which he had emerged, but he had already made himself at home in L.A. thanks to arriving with bayonets and bread trucks.

In the end, America wasn't ready to bomb its own West Coast into the Pacific when Morais was just better than they were at what had to be done. No more dissent, no more waste, just discipline and work, with occasional bread and circuses. That's how you ended up at a sugar-processing plant in Brooklyn instead of a cushy office job in midtown. You were drafted. You slept in an abandoned row house nearby.

It was the secret police that got to you. They dressed flamboyantly in spandex, external underwear, and sequined capes, like Mexican wrestlers, and took to the streets in groups of three. Most of them were American, but they all spoke Spanish or Portuguese, just to humiliate the people they were about to beat or kill with incomprehensible demands. It was the masks irked you, worse than the guns. You never even found out how many of Los Trios you killed when you spiked the sugar, or how many died when Lenny directed a charter flight off the runway and into the river. Anyone could be behind the masks. Well, anyone but Jeff, who was too thin and skeletal to ever be obscured by a wrestling getup. That's part of why everyone in the cell trusted him. Mostly it was his charisma, though.

Charisma nearly as strong as Morais's own.

And Jeff's Revolution—Mafia Style meant that he had to sway fewer people. Some bus drivers stalled out on the bridges and tunnels. One or two old school cops looted armouries. It took fewer than a dozen Con Ed workers to shut off the power, but selectively, so the hospitals could keep working. Jeff himself went down to West 18th Street and Twelfth Avenue, in the basement of the old switcher building, and took an axe to the fibre optics.

The street battles were blitzkrieg attacks. Get in, bop a few Blue Shirts or Trios, smash a window, and move on. Depend on the goodwill of the people to feed and hide you. You spent three dark days in the cellar of an old Chinese restaurant, eating nothing but handfuls of MSG. Someone would occasionally drop a leaflet or a zine full of news through the bars of the cellar window. Boston was ours again, Chicago was in flames. The heartland had taken up arms. Mexico re-annexed everything up to Colorado.

On day three you saw a pair of ratty biker boots and frayed black jeans trot by your window. Jeff. You went up to the main floor and clamoured up the fire escapes to the rooftop. It was only a five-storey walk-up (thank God for Chinatown) and you were able to follow Jeff from above. You saw him fall in that alley, but you knew it didn't matter. There were no helicopters in the air. That meant that the junta had lost the sky somehow. And they'd created a martyr in their frustration and rage.

#

Still speaking in tongues, you managed to find your way back to your own earth to at least hear what you had told the congregation. It was simple really, why the Word of Ramone had managed to unify the Earth after fifteen thousand years of civilized slaughter. Joey Ramone was a finger. A ridiculously small phalange of a great and throbbing cosmic being of near-infinite power and wisdom that scraped across the Earth when it was young, before cooling rock and quivering proteins gave rise to chance and infinite possibility. Joey Ramone was dragged across the planet, every shadow Earth in every quantum possibility, killing and fucking and feeding and inspiring and dying in an opium-induced haze, or of AIDS, or of old age. He slaughtered latter-day Hitlers in the womb or by accident of cosmic bankshots. He sang or sliced meat. He inspired the One True Faith. That's what made it easy. "We truly do have the One True Faith," you said (though you weren't sure whether you said it in English or in the verikilloanguaminesxikienima of glossolalia, but you knew they all understood you). "That's why we succeeded where all the other religions failed."

Joey Ramone saved the worlds. All of them.

#

You only met him once. You were on Third Avenue, on a day sunny enough to make the sidewalks glow. Psycho Rob was prattling in your ear.

"The next Hitler? Milosevic isn't the next fucking Hitler. There isn't one fucking next Hitler." He spat on the side of your face by mistake. Excitable boy. Then he flailed his arms and accidentally smacked you in the chest.

"Rob, fuckin' relax for a minute. You're like the Special Olympics forensics team here," you said.

He turned to you, all blue eyes and ratty blond whiskers and curls. "No man. See, what I mean is this. I think we're ALL the next Hitler. It's just that you need the right ingredients all in place, everything has to go right—well, everything has to go wrong for the next Hitler to really be the next Hitler." He spun on the heel of his tennis shoe and pointed.

"That old lady," he said, nodding and jabbing his finger. "She's the next Hitler." It was an old, probably Chinese, woman in a floral blouse. She was standing on a traffic island, waiting to pull her granny cart across the street.

"That is an old lady. She has a hump. She can barely move. She is not Hitler."

"Hitler," Rob said, defiant. "All it takes is a little of this and a little of that. That old lady could lead a rally in Chinatown and have one hundred thousand people ready to die for her tomorrow. If she wasn't a hunchback, maybe her charisma would be enough to split the world down the middle. Osteoporosis may have saved us all!" He turned and looked over his shoulder at you, then shut his eyes dramatically. "Anyone!" he shouted, "can be a Hitler!" And, eyes still closed, he spun again with his arm and forefinger outstretched, and pointed.

At Joey Ramone. Joey had just turned the corner and was nursing a big McDonalds cola. His hair was shorter in that it was all piled at the top of his head, and didn't flow down his back. Black streaked with a thread or two of silver. Purple Lennon glasses, and a nerdy shirt with horizontal stripes and a crooked collar. He had a paunch but that was it—four pipe cleaners sticking out of a ball of clay. The world stopped for a moment, like it does when non-New Yorkers see celebrities. You had rolled your eyes at Sandra Bernhardt buying deli flowers at midnight, and didn't even recognize Leonard Cohen when he bought the *Times* at the newsstand. The girl you were with just turned the corner and left after you admitted that.

But Joey you just stared at. His shadow was half a block long. "Hi guys," he said, and he walked past you and Rob both to cross the street. You just smiled back. The old lady eyed him warily, then smiled a wide toothless smile.

The Dead Don't Stay Dead

Edgar Allan Poe's New York

Edgar Allan Poe spent most of his adult life chasing the phantoms of fame and fortune up and down the Northeast Corridor. More than once he came to New York to make a name for himself, but for the most part Poe lived in utter poverty and scribbled for a variety of forgotten periodicals. He did get a taste of the city's renowned literary salons and even launched a one-sided war against the poet Longfellow to try to puff his own reputation, but it was all for nothing. Poe borrowed money fruitlessly, got drunk constantly, and fell to pieces on the street more than once. The glory Manhattan promised was always one big deal away.

Stop me if this sounds familiar.

There's not much left of Poe's New York, which consisted of over ten addresses in Manhattan and the Bronx. Poe was po', after all, and ended up shuffling his little family of wife and mother-in-law from boarding house to boarding house, farm to tenement, apartment to cottage. New York University recently tore down the building Poe lived in at 85 West 3rd Street to expand its law school's digs, over the complaints of preservationists and fans. An editorial in the law school's paper said that the Poe building was "about as much a landmark as Gray's Papaya."

Poe's addresses on Carmine and Greenwich Streets have long since been demolished and rebuilt. The Northern Dispensary on the corner of Waverly Place and Waverly Place (really, check out the street sign!), where the poet went to get his headaches treated, still stands, but that's it for buildings in Manhattan. While a Manhattanite, Poe was once found wandering in a drunken fugue across the Hudson, in the woods beyond Jersey City. Even those trees are long gone.

In the Bronx, however, stands the Poe Cottage, only a few yards from the Kingsbridge Road subway stop and on the wrong side of the Wall of Nonexistent Negro Hordes that keep nervous white folk away from the borough. Poe moved up to what was then the country in 1846 in a last-ditch attempt to keep his wife Virginia, who spent more of her life dying than living, from succumbing to tuberculosis. She died in the cottage, in the bed still on display.

The Cottage is only open on the weekends. You'll have to squint to get a glimpse of Poe's privation—I couldn't help but think "Dude! Duplex!" when I walked in. The rooms are tiny and ceilings low, but a cottage like this, if it could even exist in the concrete jungle of the 21st century, would easily rent for five grand a month. Poe paid $100 per year. It cost me three bucks just to see the five rooms.

The Cottage is all but ignored, though it stands proud and clean in the city's neat little Poe Park. On the day I went, the caretaker, who actually lives in the cottage (ssshhh, don't tell), mentioned that we were the only tourists that day. Poe wrote "The Bells" there, a complaint in verse about the church bells at St. John's College, now Fordham University. "Annabel Lee" too. Plus a few other things most New York junior high school students spend a few weeks sweating over. And nobody seems to care.

Why should the modern-day New Yorker care about Edgar Allan Poe, 169 years later? Mainly because he was right. While his contemporaries the Transcendentalists were writing about individualism and communing with nature in the wide open spaces of the frontier, Poe's stories were all about being walled into buildings, being besieged by crime and madmen, and the inmates who ran the asylums. The dead never stayed dead in Poe's tales or poems, their memories hid behind every corner and in every shadow.

Stop me if this sounds familiar. The cramped apartments, the wilting shrines to the victims of 9/11, the greedy hustles for cash and literary immortality (raise your hand if you're working on a novel), all prove that we still live in Poe's New York.

Poe wasn't just an old ghost story teller. He invented the modern detective story, after all. Poe's sleuth Auguste Dupin struggled with the new cityscapes just as Poe did—his exploits confronted the ability of industrial urbanism to destroy the individual. It's easy to disappear without a trace in a sprawling human zoo, like poor Marie Roget did in Poe's famous tale.

Poe vanished too when he left New York, on the verge of finally founding his own magazine, *The Stylus*, which he was sure would make his fortune. Instead he reappeared a week later, horrifically drunk and in clothes not his own, outside of a Baltimore polling place. Tortured by delusions and phantasms, it took him several days to die.

But Poe didn't stay dead. His reputation grew and he's now considered the most important American writer ever. And even though there isn't an edifice left in Manhattan that Poe would know as his home, there is one more place to visit. West 84th Street is also known as Edgar Allan Poe Street. Poe lived in one of the tiny houses surrounding the Brennen Mansion that once stood on West 84th and Broadway. Nearby is Café Edgar's. Don't go there, it is too expensive, but do press your nose up against the window, as the social climbing-yet-hungry Poe himself might have had to do.

Then walk into Riverside Park and find the close by outcropping of rocks. You'll be standing atop "Mount Tom." We don't know whether Mount Tom is an ironic name or a reference to the way the rocks, when covered in snow, looks like a sheep's ass, but have a seat anyway. Face west. Look out at the Hudson River. Bring a notebook, just like Poe did. Before there was a West Side Highway. Before the high rises of Guttenberg and West New York. This is where Poe spent his days while he wrote his most famous work of all, "The Raven." Then die a mediocrity and wait while the city is demolished and rebuilt half-a-dozen times over. Maybe, just maybe, your New York will be remembered, because in this town, the dead don't stay dead.

That's my plan, anyway.

February 2003.

Beer On Sunday

The day after the Rapture, Tommy goes looking for his bookie Newsboy Shaw, but he isn't nowhere to be found. He ain't in the park and weren't loitering by the newsstand neither. And that's really a hangnail because Tommy bet 318 on the numbers after he heard that the old 318 derailed and blew up in the ditch after her conductor got called home by Jesus. So did all the other boys in town, so if Tommy don't find Newsboy soon, he's gonna be left with but moths in his purse.

I spy Tommy through the window and rap on the glass for him to come have a sip and he turns and grins and comes on in and takes a seat next to Father Beef who has been here all morning even though I caught him diddling my boy Roy but two years yesterday. Tommy ponies up to the bar and just gives me the hairy eyeball tills I tell him it is okay cuz the blue laws got Hoovered up to heaven with all the churchmice except Father Beef, the ol' baby effer. Beef just looks down into his little glass of sloe gin fizz and Tommy smiles and takes a pint.

"So," Beef is telling me in his little steampipe mary voice, "I placed three dollars on 479 but it dint came up. 479 is the school what's still burning," he says. I say I can still smell it and that he better not think of schools anyway if he is all down here with the rest of us for the next seven years like he's sayin' he's to be. Tommy asks after my wife and I tell him she's gone to Jesus and that is why he gets beer on Sunday now instead of a frying pan to the bean and we laughed and then we all duck cuz someone is on the nut and trying to blast the sky with a tommygun but the bullets just keep hitting us poor bastards.

"Goddamn, where are the John Law I know they ain't been took up to heaven, those murdering bulls," Tommy says and I says yeah, but they might be cops doing all the shooting up because they have no reason not to just shoot on any mac who wanders by we all being disgraceful sinners and all. Beef says this is hell on earth and Tommy says it aint's cuz he has a pint and his mother-in-law gone missing too and we all laugh at that.

"Put it on my tab," Tommy says and I makes a face like the devil but he just laughs and says what am I to do, call John Law and I says I can brain him good with my ballbat. Tommy says I can trust him because he won big on the numbers with ol' 318, while sticks like Beef here was playing 479. I say that ain't the only thing Beef was playing and I get all mad again about my boy Roy whose shorts been all bloody but Beef looks so sad like a woman or a white prune that I can't just be pounding him and I starts to nearly cry. Tommy takes off his hat all solemn like.

"You can't do to collect on the numbers now, Tom," Beef says a little up on herself like we've gotta listen to his queeny ways, "it won't do because that number been played out. The bookmakers skips out when the big numbers hit too much. All Newark plays either 318 or 479 yesterday and even if half of em been taken by Our Lord ain't nobody will pay out. You bets on a broke bank you get broke."

Tommy just shakes his head and says, "No no, not Newsboy. He's honest aces—a real narrow arrow. He even pays when the rest of the books head for the hills. Right McGinty?" he looks at me and I says yes sir because it is true. Newsboy's an honest abe and that's how I founded this fine establishment. Because I picked 114 after the big 114 flophouse fired up and he pays out to everybody even if the other books make like a drum and beat it.

"He's honest then," Beef says, he's a real egghead now, "but nobody else is, so what makes you think the money is any good?"

And Tommy ain't hep to it because he is on the relief but I does suddenly, because Banker Sprague is a regular Charlie Churchmouse and he been took and lots of other mugs were too. The President also flew out of here and the Supreme Court too and if there ain't no government and banks than the money in the till ain't worth what I was the day I am born. That's my acumen he's messed with now and I just want to pound that old B. F. again but I sees he's crying now so I let him be.

And Tommy says how will he pay his tab and I say gold and proves it by snatching up Father Beef's crucifix from right around his chicken-neck. He says but I gave you First Communion and I says yeah and I still got my communion money saved in a mason jar but it ain't worth TP. Then Beef, he gets all up like he wants me to knock him down but then the air turns red and the frogs start falling like hail thumping on the cars and windows outside so we scram for the back room with our cocktails.

And for a time we don't say nothing because there ain't much to conversate about other than the smell and the howling and the devils in the shadows and how we got seven years of this hell on earth till we get to hell on hell on a shingle herself.

"This is Babylon, sons," Beef says to Tommy after a think. "And penny-ante players like you can't be no crook in a world of crooks. God ain't had to do nothing but leave us all here to wait for our depraved natures to take us down. There ain't never will be no more handshake deals no more cross your heart and hope to die. And ain't no more swears on your mother's grave, because she's leaving it presently to be with Jesus and Mary neither." And Beef opens up to say something more but then he just starts sobbing all over again and Tommy looks at me and he shrugs.

"You seen Newsboy, McGinty?" he asks me and I says no, because Newsboy is a teetotaler so he never has no business in here anyhow unless its cards and it ain't been cards on Sunday yet. Tommy looks over to the cards table and sees all the drapes that got left behind when the game was broke up yesterday by the clouds and the sunbeam and the angel choir taking two of the boys home and Tommy runs over and starts going through the pockets but I already Hooverized it all.

"Oh man alive, what if Newsboy got him a call to the Lord," Tommy says and he looks at Beef because Beef knows the Good Word even if he didn't follow it which is why he's here drinking on Sunday and why my sweet Roy is just listening at the radio all day but Beef shakes his head.

"Newsboy Shaw is a cut throat, a footpad and a gambler and he dint even marry his girl but for the judge not before God. He must be here or if he ain't then he's playing cards with old Scratch if he got plugged this very morning," Beef says. "After all, if I did not get called home," he starts up but then stops for I was looking at him. What do you know anyway, I ask him. Not a goddamn thing, I tell him.

'Well, goddamn it all to hell," Tommy says and he walks back to holding up the wall. "My ships all come in and the dock's been rooked," and then he tells me he wants to have my wheelbarrow to be collecting all the clothes and maybe he can sell him for his nut and I say he can but that's just fool because there's lots more clothes than people now damn this pious little burg. Supply and demand is what I know from better than Newsboy Shaw does. Nobody won't be buying nothing they can find on the streets free as frogs.

And then Tommy's beer turns to blood and he throws it up and it's all full of worms and little white maggots and I say this is getting out of hands here and Beef says it is because beer on Sunday is still a sin and the Lord don't need to test us no more because He got us right where he wants 'em. I has enough and clocks the little baby effer finally and he falls right over. I tell Tommy I'll go up and get him another beer and most of it is all wormy too but for the Guinness because the Lord is merciful so I pull one for Tommy but spills it when I see them all at my windows clawing and scratching.

White boys like they was drowned staring to get in. Them eyes red as stoplights but squinty too. Then they bust through my window and start coming for me and I wave Beef's cross but it don't do no good and I call for Tommy and he comes out and they dogpile on him. I gets my ballbat from the bar and start cracking at 'em all. It's like smacking mudball after mudball except white and smelly like the pier in summer.

Ol' Tommy manages to get a chair and breaks it over the little bastards. He's a tall drink of water so he's wading through them and I see they've been the kids from the tb ward but the ones that died all on the last year or so and I hoist many a stein in their honor with their old dads but they don't care and I bats them down good till they're all down for the count.

And Father Beef, his head a lump, comes out maybe because he can smell little boy and starts crying and he says he'd have killed himself already but this ain't nothing compared to the hell that awaits and I look around my establishment and tend to agree. Then I remember the Guinness and pull another round for my poor ol' boys and give them the guns I took off the chairs when Sweet Jesus took away the Sarge and his card night boys.

Beef ain't never used a gun but I can tell he used a beer as he drinks it right down and then taps on the glass like a queen for another but I pull him one anyway in case he can make his cross work better than your truly could have in account I ain't even been in church since Roy was six and Beef did him. Roy's eight now, like the boys splattering up my tables, but he's a good boy he's just stuck down here with the rest of us on account of Father Beef but I pour him a beer anyhow.

And Tommy says I should hire him as a bull so as to keep the devil's riff-raff out and I could pay him in Guinness if I can keep the supply up and I start to give it a think about what I can trade for more of the stuff, if the route is even still up after yesterday. Ol' William the teamster was a pious sort after all, he may be gone to heaven and have a new route up there after all, but Beef says that if the one true draft is still good than the Lord is still merciful and I tells Tommy I'll think about it. Then we hear the glass outside crunching all quiet like.

Tommy waves me back and he gets to crouching down behind an overturned table and has his little heater out. Father Beef just backs up with his mug and Tommy's too and is sippin' from them round robin—one from his, one two from Tommy's and he's practically in the back room again but still looking. I got one hand on my pistol and the other on my bat and we hear the glassy walking getting a little louder and a long wheeze like a kid with the cough and I starts to feel my courage leak out of me, I'm shamed to say. But not for me, see, but for poor ol' Roy. I bets the radio will stop working soon and he's going to cry for his mama again but there won't be no mama or no pa and nobody to help him in this lonely world and that just gets me riled up and I swear I'm set to shoot the Devil himself if he darkened my door but it wasn't the devil it was Kuncklebone Shaw, Newsboy's no-account brother. He's Newsboy's muscle, but it's all in his head, see?

I just laugh at him then because Knucklebone doffs his hat like he's courting us and steps on a frog and just keeps coming in. "H'lo

McGinty," he says to me, but slow, slow being the way he is. He don't come up to a stool but just looks around at the whitewash dead boys we broke and says to me if I've seen Tommy and I nod over and Tommy stands up with his piece still out but pointed right at Knucklebone's head, which is only aiming to improve Knucklebone's noggin' anyhow.

But Knucklebone just strides on up like the gun was licorice or something. He puts his cap back on and pulls out a kerchief from his pocket and unwraps it and I see a little notebook and some shiny pebbles and Knucklebone reads "Tom Reed, five dollars on 318 for today," like he was asking. And Tommy puts down his piece and takes out his ticket and Knucklebone reads the ticket real slow like 318 is some big sum and then nods and hands over Tommy the kerchief and he walks out with the ticket in both of his big ham hands like it is his fortune on there.

And Tommy looks at the kerchief and laughs out loud, real real loud. And Beef swishes up to him and asks what is it son and I look over too because I can use a laugh and Tommy says look and puts out his hand and I do.

And it is gold. Gold fillings, right from the jaw of Newsboy Shaw, whose been such the honest bookmaker that he got called home and left ain't nothing but he was born with behind, like golden fillings enough to pay off his debt to ol' Tommy. And we're all laughing at this and then ol' Jack comes in with Newsboy's shiny watch what Knucklebone gave him and then here comes Trudy with a pretty swank set of golden cuffs also from Knucklebone, who got himself left behind because of Father Beef the baby effer I guess and I pull them all drafts because it is still Sunday and God is still merciful, and beer is but our sacrament.

How to Rid the World of Good

On September 11, 2001, two airliners crashed into the Twin Towers of New York City's World Trade Center, obliterating the buildings and killing thousands of working people, tourists, executives, and passers-by. A third plane crashed into the Pentagon, killing a couple hundred more people, and a fourth plane crash-landed in Pennsylvania, presumably short of its target somewhere in Washington, DC. At press time, this unprecedented disaster was believed to be the work of terrorists under the aegis of Osama bin Laden, the Saudi millionaire and former CIA asset. [1] The perceptual reaction was swift. The terrorists were evil, perhaps evil lunatics, who attacked the US only because of a hatred of freedom, a jealousy of the United States' way of life. The US, victim of this attack, was good. President George W. Bush was explicit: "This will be a monumental struggle of good versus evil," he explained to the shocked nation. The little AOL news zipper was even more succinct: "Bush promises to 'rid world of evil.'"

"Good versus evil" was shorthand obscuring all the complexities of the last fifty years of US foreign policy in the Middle East and the near-inevitable "blowback" of the September 11 attacks. The very notion of good versus evil is not an artifact of material reality (there is neither good nor evil in the real world), nor is it some deep, hardwired set of archetypes squirming around the human brain. Ironically enough, it is an artifact of the Persian domination of the cradle of civilization, and this apocalyptic worldview that so neatly splits all experience, thought, and imagination into two categories has been with the Western world ever since. So it wasn't always like this. Many of the greatest works of antiquity, for example, do not involve the conflict between good and evil. The epic poems and tragedies of ancient Greece are not concerned with such a struggle, and even the earliest books of the Bible posit evil as an overdetermined force—God, through a variety of agents, creates evil as an obstacle or mile marker on a path toward a closer relationship with the Divine.

In Homer's *Illiad*, Hektor, the breaker of horses and the hero of Troy, was as respected and admired, and as much of a protagonist, as any of the Greek heroes. In *Odyssey*, the capriciousness of the gods was not a reflection of their evil, and Odysseus was neither good nor evil in his attempts to stay alive and get home to Ithaca. He was simply noble, intelligent, wise, crafty, and wily; the best a human being could be. He manifested *arete.* [2]

Further, good and evil as we know them don't appear as concepts in any work by Sophocles, Euripides, or Aeschylus. Good does not rise up and conquer evil; evil is not inexplicable, animal, unfair, or inescapable. Even in *The Eumenides*, which features the Greek spirits of vengeance, the Furies, there is no final apocalyptic conflict between good and evil. Instead, the Furies are encouraged to turn Orestes, who killed his mother, over to Athenian judges for trial. Athena declares Orestes acquitted and then turns to the Furies themselves. She asks them to end their bitterness and live with her as goddesses. She will bear their anger and their role, and she asks them not to infect the hearts of young men with evil and the thirst for revenge.

She tells them, "Do good, receive good, and be honored as the good are honored. Share our country, the beloved of god." [3] Initially, the Furies balk at this request, and repeat their old grievances against the new gods and their commitment to reason, and threaten to punish the land. Athena continues reasoning with the Furies, offering them both the classic carrot—offerings from the people—and the stick—the wrath of Zeus and his thunderbolts. The Furies initially don't believe that the people of Athens could ever accept them as part of the civil society of democracy, rather than as symbols of vengeance and fear, but Athena convinces them otherwise through logical argument and personal empathy.

In Aeschylus' worldview, the ferocity of the Furies can be integrated into a peaceful society, and the primal nature of emotion can be reconciled into the world of reason without being cast out or destroyed. This is done through the democratic process and through reasoned debate between equals—there is no apocalyptic battle, no utter destruction or negation of the primitive side of human nature, and no essentialist arguments about the nature of good and evil. And indeed, the Furies finally accept Athena's offer and become Eumenides, or the kindly ones, whose mission is to keep Athens from civil war and to provide prosperity and blessings for the democracy.

The notion of good versus evil as the underlying theme of some *übernarrative* that informs all human thought and behavior cannot be found even in the earliest books of the Old Testament, the foundation of Judeo-Christian mythology. The "original sin" of Adam and Eve was a relatively late invention, and understandably so. One needn't be a theologian to point to the massive plot and consistency holes in the well-known story of Man's Fall. Why was the fruit in the Garden? Why would God allow the serpent into the Garden? Isn't knowledge a good thing, and if so, why would God prevent eating from the Tree of Knowledge? There are many explanations, and the earliest don't use the concept of good versus evil. "One source assures us that [the serpent] was the angels' emissary; they had concluded that man would represent too formidable a challenge unless he could be made to stray and sin."[4] In other legendary Jewish commentaries—the texts of the Midrash—surrounding the event, "Adam and Eve *had* to defy God so that their descendants might sing His praises." [5]

What about the serpent? Wasn't he the Devil in disguise, looking to tempt the unwary and thwart the (necessarily) good plans of God? Not necessarily. Much of the Old Testament, including the entire Book of Job, shows Satan (and, more generally, satans) as an angel with a special task, that of obstacle. "The root *stn* means 'one who opposes, obstructs, or acts as adversary.' (The Greek term *diabolos*, later translated 'devil,' literally means 'one who throws something across one's path.')" [6] And the obstacle doesn't necessarily take the form of a test or temptation, either; Satan appears in some stories in order to be an obstacle on the path to some event or circumstance. And if the path or circumstance is bad, then the obstacle is beneficial.

The etymology of *diabolos* provides further clues. "Devil" isn't quite a translation of *diabolos*; it has even older roots:

> The Devas of the [Hindu] Veda are the bright gods who fight on the side of Indra; in the [Zoroastrian] Avesta the word has come to mean an evil spirit, and the Zoroastrian was bound to declare that he ceased to be a worshipper of the daevas . . .
>
> [T]he word devil passed into an immense number of forms, the Gothic *tieval*, *diuval*, *diufal*, the Icelandic *djofull*, Swedish *djevful*, all of them, together with the Italian, French, and Spanish forms carrying back the word διαβολος [diabolos] to the same root which furnished the Latin *Divus*, *Djovis*, and the Sanskrit *deva*. [7]

The word "demon" has some noble ancestors, as well. In Greek, the *daemon* was the divine force that engendered and informed the character of men (women had their own spirits). In Latin, this concept was adopted and called *genius*. The genius was eventually separated from the self as a concept and was identified with household gods and ancestral spirits, the Manes.[8] *Daemon* was well-known enough as a term describing an internal creative spirit, or as a set of natural skills and inclinations, to make it into Shakespeare, as per this discussion between an Egyptian seer and Antony:

> Thy daemon, that thy spirit which keeps thee, is Noble, courageous, high, unmatchable, Where Caesar's is not. But near him thy angel Becomes afeard, as being o'erpowered.
>
> (*Antony and Cleopatra* 2.3.17-20)

The inclusion of artifacts of the personality within the greater rubric of evil also suggests that some transcultural, transhistorical fear of the Other is not to blame for the modern ubiquity of good/evil narratives. Before the good/evil split, it wasn't unusual for the Other to be widely respected, up to and including adopting gods and heroes from neighboring cultures, incorporating them into the local pantheon. As seen in Homer, it was simple enough to have an extensive, bloody war with a neighboring kingdom, with little more than freely admitted acrimony over property and honor at stake; all the Greek and Trojan heroes were fully realized as human beings with human drives and circumstances. The Trojans are not dehumanized as the Other.

The Bible isn't even consistent on who the Other is and what its role was, even up to offering different agents of change for different accounts of the same incident. In 2 Samuel 24, for example, God influences David to take a census, then punishes him for doing so. In 1 Chronicles 21:1, the same event is described, with one difference. Rather than God directly influencing David's behavior, and then unleashing a plague, an evil emissary is credited with having David take the forbidden census. Chronicles, written about a century after Samuel, still doesn't demonstrate a good/evil duality. Rather, God performs evil actions indirectly. In neither case, it should be noted, is evil in opposition to good. Both work hand-in-hand to achieve a natural and ultimately good result, namely the will of God.

The Persian occupation, circa the fifth century BCE, led to interaction between Judaism and Zoroastrianism, and the duality of the latter religion—plus other concepts, like angels and the immortality of the soul—was picked up from Zoroastrianism by Jewish sects.[9] Founded by the Persian prophet Zarathustra, Zoroastrianism offered a monotheistic creed to a polytheistic region. The religion posits a single, all-powerful god, Ahura Mazda, who created the material world and communicated with humanity via the Amesha Spentas, the personifications of certain abstract concepts. Angra Mainyu, the hostile spirit, is a finite, evil being who brought ruin, death, and destruction upon the material world, but who will eventually be destroyed through the good actions of human beings. Additionally, Zoroastrianism posits the eventual arrival of a savior, Saoshyant, who will be born of a virgin. This savior will raise the dead and lead them all to a final judgment.

Sound familiar? One or more of the Jewish sects impacted by Zoroastrianism happened to become Christianity, which eventually took over most of the world. And indeed, it was Christianity that put the final nail in the coffin of religious pluralism. Clement of Alexandria declared, contra the practice of Roman paganism and most of the public cults of the day, that "the gods of all the nations are images of demons."[10] Previously, the commonalties of neighboring pantheons were highlighted, and most worshippers assumed that foreign gods were variants on their local gods.

Once Christianity became the public cult, the success of the good/evil dichotomy in both explaining the natural world and in creating cross-ethnic unity across Christendom was quite handy. If illness and disaster were the work of the Devil, the victims could be blamed for their own misfortune, since God would clearly protect them otherwise. The successful, of course, were owed their success thanks to their piety. Evil was then applied to certain other cultural groups in order to limit trade, encourage war-making, engage in land grabs, and undercut internal ethnic communities that might have had foreign allegiances. The strategy of obscure Iranian prophets had made the big time.

Today the secular world doesn't need Satan. Good and evil, however, are in great demand. The old Iranian dualism of good versus evil is entirely an arbitrary one, but it's effective for maintaining social order. In US history, the good/evil dualism was projected onto the continent itself. The undiscovered countries of Africa and North America were cast in the role of evil, conveniently enough, as they were both un-Christian and ripe for exploration and exploitation in a way that much of seventeenth-century Asia was not. In 1676, Bacon's Rebellion, which saw both black and white indentured servants rise up against their masters, threatened the power of the fledgling Virginia colony and led directly to the "divide and conquer" strategy that split poor whites from poor blacks politically, socially, and spiritually. Poor whites were favored over blacks and granted a level of citizenship (an arbitrary concept that boils down to, "You are within this set of dotted lines and you are good.") that put them on the good side of the dualism of Christianity/savagery, white/black, and worker/slave.

This dualism also informed the slavery of blacks in the United States for the next two centuries, as well as the three centuries of genocide of various Native American tribes in the continental United States and Hawaii. The United States also emerged as a world power and used its newfound influence over the West's mass culture to offer a thoroughly revisionist history of both slavery and the Indian Wars through popular fiction and motion pictures. This same revisionism can be found across fiction generally; everything from the hundreds of Tolkien-inspired fantasy novels to the modern technothriller utilize the same duality of the Western frontier combat narrative. The Western itself was in turn influenced by the heroic Romances, which had the explicit lessons of the good/evil duality as their primary thematic/narrative goal. [11]

This dualism now informs the Muslim world as the propaganda enemy of the United States. Currently, the United States is bombing the already shattered landscape of Afghanistan in order to root out the ruling Taliban and find the arch-terrorist and media-proclaimed "evil mastermind" Osama bin Laden. At the same time, anonymous individuals are sending anthrax-tainted materials through the mails to government officials and media outlets. At the time of this writing, the terror campaigns of (presumably) bin Laden and the anthrax letters are widely considered to be linked, but the reactions to the two elements of terrorism are entirely divorced.

It is publicly acknowledged that most Afghans are "innocent" in that they support neither the Taliban nor Osama bin Laden. Decades of war and interventions by both the United States and the USSR have left the country shattered. Accompanying the US bombing runs are food drops, which have been roundly criticized by most observers as a simple propaganda move, and a White House fundraising scheme wherein American children are asked to send dollar bills to the White House in order to feed Afghan children. [12] These moves are tactical media events, not real attempts to ease the suffering of the Afghan people. Rather, they exist to ensure the United States public that they are on the side of good.

The vast majority of people in Afghanistan are innocent, but in order to root out the evil bin Laden's hiding place (which may not even be in Afghanistan), they must suffer through terrible bombings. The US is also hiding parts of bin Laden's terror network, as can be seen by the existence of our anonymous Anthrax Mary and his or her (or their) busy mailing campaign. And yet, the United States is not bombing parts of Florida or Trenton, New Jersey, much less Texas-sized areas around these locations.

Both the Afghans and the Americans are equally innocent.

But only one is "good." Only one exists within the magic circle. The Afghans need not be guilty for the United States government, and much of the American public, to chalk up their despair to poor luck or the sacrifices that one (typically someone else) needs to make in order for good to triumph over evil. The United States and its citizens, inherently good, intrinsically innocent, and in a blessed, free land, are immune from the consequences of their actions. It was George W. Bush who coined the phrase-cum-demand, "May God continue to bless America," at about the same time that he swore to "rid the world of evil." And thanks to a long-ago Iranian prophet, even the slaughter of the universally-acknowledged innocent can be called good. The recognition of the false duality that allows innocent deaths to be called good should be sufficient, dear reader, to allow the good to fold in on itself and disappear in a puff of logic. Consider yourself liberated.

Won't go very far toward eliminating the evil, however.

October 2001

Endnotes

1. In 1987 alone, the US government gave Afghani terrorists-cum-freedom fighters $500 million, and bin Laden and his Saudi allies matched this largesse dollar for dollar. See Weaver, Mary Anne. "The Real bin Laden." *The New Yorker* 24 Jan, 2000: 32.

2. Manifesting *arete* is a tricky thing to write, because arete is a tricky concept to grasp. Generally, the concept of *eudaimonia,* following Aristotle, refers to the constant, excellent activity of those parts of the soul that are peculiar to human beings. However, since the soul is ineffable, the only way to be aware of this excellence is to observe it in other human beings. *Arete* refers both to excellence in taking actions dictated by reason, and a variety of virtues (moderation, courage, practical wisdom, etc.) that are developed through habit, not through nature. *Arete,* is thus "excellence of being" and is conceptually designed to replace simple pleasure as the goal of life. Needless to say, English

doesn't have a word for this concept.

3. Aeschylus, *The Eumenides.* Tr. Richmond Lattimore, 868-9.

4 .Wiesel, Elie. *Messengers of God.* New York: Simon and Schuster (A Touchstone Book), 1994: 17.

5. *Ibid.*: 27.

6. Pagels, Elaine. *The Origin of Satan.* New York: Random House, 1995: 39-41.

7.Cox, George. *Mythology of the Aryan Nations.* Longmans, 1870: 355, 363.

8. Remember those really weak devils from Dungeons & Dragons? That's them.

9. For more on this incredibly complex subject and the roots of Zarathustra's own ideas of good/evil duality and how they relate to Hinduism and its spread thanks to the Indo-European invasion of circa 2000 BCE, check out Messandé , G. *The History of the Devil.* London: Newleaf, 1986.

10. *Ibid.*: 262.

11. For a further discussion of genre as an outgrowth of the Romantic period, see: Olsen, Lance. *Rebel Yell: A Short Guide to Fiction Writing.* Cambrian Publications, 1998.

12. Afghanistan has several million starving residents, many of whom were being fed by a variety of relief organizations until the bombing began. The airdrops of individual Meals Ready to Eat would not provide sustenance for even a tenth of the people in need in Afghanistan, even if every meal landed on the lap of a starving person. Additionally, most of the food is being dropped in the best-fed area in

the country; there is no infrastructure on the ground to collect and distribute the food; and much of the food is landing in minefields. As far as the cash to Afghan children, the notion of converting a pile of dollar bills into useful funds for Afghan children and only Afghan children, most of whom do not participate in a cash economy, should be obviously foolish to even the densest observer.

The Birth of Western Civilization

Black smoke from the burning hunks of oxen drifted up towards the fog-shrouded peaks of Mount Olympus. In the temple, one of the citizens led a murmured prayer while his slaves and young son looked on. Zeus was not on Olympus to smell the sweet aroma of meats given in sacrifice. His dead body rested in a ditch outside a small home on the outskirts of Athens.

"Now what are we going to do?" asked Philippius.

"All I know is that I know nothing," Socrates said. The old man kicked Zeus's carcass with a satisfying thump. "What are we going to do?" he asked himself as he looked about to make sure nobody was watching.

It began earlier that evening. Socrates was finishing up a day's lessons with Philippius and a few other students. The sun was high in the air and hot. It hadn't rained in three weeks. Brown and green grass crunched under Socrates's feet as he wove his way through the clump of young men sitting around him. They were spread out on the rise of a small hill, their skin glistening and muscles tense under their tunics. Socrates wore a longer robe; it trailed behind him as he paced.

"But Teacher, how can having few possessions bring one closer to the gods if the gods themselves are given to finery? The Apollonian temple itself must store dozens of golden and silver tripod stools," asked Xanthus, a dark-haired boy.

"Yes, yes," added Philippius, nodding and taking up the thread of the idea. "And how can you reconcile this statement with your statement that the gods themselves are naught more than the idle thoughts of frightened men?"

Socrates nodded seriously, his wiry gray beard brushing his chest as he peered at his toes. His nails were thick and white and his soles and ankles stained green from the fresh grass he had been walking through.

"Good questions, good questions all. How do you think I know these things? Do you think I should even try to reconcile those statements? What is the nature of the gods?" he asked Philippius, stripping the boy of his tunic with his eyes. The old man wondered if his student's stomach was lean and taut or round from rich food. He determined to find out.

"I'm not sure, teacher, that is why I asked," said Xanthus. Socrates ignored him entirely, having already had him some weeks ago.

"Philippius, are the gods held to contract?"

Philippius blinked and sat up. "Well, I don't know."

"Do they meet their obligations?"

"Well . . . " the young man said tentatively, "we try to win their favor, but they remain capricious."

"And who are the most capricious mortals?"

"Children and the idle rich."

"And what don't children and the idle rich have?"

"Many financial obligations," said Xanthus triumphantly. Socrates and the other students glared at him. Philippius even dug up a small pebble from the dirt and flung it at the boy's head. In a flash they were both on their feet. Philippius ducked his blond head down and tackled Xanthus. Xanthus wrapped his dark arms around Philippius's neck and back, twisting him into a three-quarters nelson. Soon the other boys were up, cheering and kicking the tangle of bodies when they could. The philosopher grabbed a downed branch and strode in, swinging blindly.

"Stop, stop!" he cried out, whipping everyone in sight. The stick snapped in his hand and he fell into the pile of student bodies as a few older women down in the marketplace called up at the gang of kids.

"What's going on? Leave that man alone!"

"Barbarians! Spartans! Acting like dogs! Acting like slaves!"

Philippius up-ended Xanthus finally, but got a forearm to the jaw for his trouble. Finally, the old master and the other boys managed to pull the two apart. Philippius ended up in Socrates's lap, the old man's arms cinched tightly around his waist. Panting heavily and sweating, Socrates dragged the boy to his feet, but kept the embrace locked. Two other boys had secured Xanthus, holding his arms wide.

"And what was that all about?" demanded Socrates. "Are you all so eager for the slightest recognition that you'll attract the greatest recognition of all, that of public spectacle?" Socrates swung his chin to point at the group of women at the base of the hill. They had gone from yelling to simply pointing and laughing. A few clucked their tongues and then went back to their stalls.

"Even the slave women were mocking you." He pushed Philippius forward, letting go of his grip violently. "You may all go."

As the students skulked away, Socrates reached out and put a strong hand on the blond boy's shoulder.

"Boy, come home with me tonight. Let us dine together. Go to the market and buy us some sausage and cheese. You may spend the evening as well."

Philippius smiled, relieved. "Yes teacher. I'll spend two obols and get the best sausage they have!"

"Better make it three obols," Socrates said, furrowing his brow. "I'm quite hungry."

The boy nodded and ran down the hill. Socrates followed slowly, picking his way down the steep incline. He passed Xanthus, who was resting in the shade of a tree near the market.

"Hypocrite," the boy hissed, knowing that the breeze would carry the word to the old man's ears.

On high Olympus, Zeus was looking for his sandals. A bevy of air spirits, whirling and whooshing through the pillars that held up the sky, were looking for them as well. A zephyr spun a pair of sandals through the air, landing them at the Zeus's feet. Zeus slipped on a few torn rags and turned his hair from fiery red to gray with a thought.

"And where precisely do you think you are going?" a voice like ten thousand chickenhawks screamed. The marble floors curdled at the voice. It was Hera, Zeus's wife.

"Out! Out and away! To walk the world like a mortal man! And mortal men do not need to answer to their hearth-bound wives!" the god thundered. The clouds went gray and black as his voice echoed across the sky. Zeus cringed and hoped the display would work.

It didn't. "What? Don't you dare compare me to one of those fleshy specks of time and dust!" Hera shouted. Her face was flush, reddening like cheap wine.

Zeus slowly turned on his heels, letting his gritted teeth relax and his cringe unwind to his full posture. "My love, please. A man needs to go out. I cannot be so isolated from our people. Some of them are beginning to get some ideas. Strange ideas."

Hera stood her ground, hands on her hips. "Oh?"

Zeus nodded and said in his softest, gravest voice, "Yes, atheism." He slowly began to ease backwards.

Hera gaped, "Impossible! What a ludicrous idea. You should unleash the great waters again, and drown that planet full of arrogant bastards. That would teach them the folly of hubris. A field trip won't."

"I know. But I also want to get drunk." With that Zeus threw himself backwards and transformed himself into a lightning bolt. He ripped through the sky to the ground, leaving his wife howling. The wind swore in rage.

At his home Socrates peered out the window as he was washed by a young slave.

"Did you hear a thunder stroke?"

"No, master," said the girl, pouring another jug of water over her master's head.

Philippius walked past the portico with a basket of food. "Teacher!" he called out. Socrates waved his slave to collect the basket and wrapped a cloth around himself.

"I hope I'm not late?"

"No, no, not at all," Socrates murmured as he walked into the small white serving room. He stretched on his couch as the young girl set down a plate of cheese and great blue grapes. Socrates tugged on the girl's dark hair. "Thank you. Go now and bring wine. Cook those sausages too. Take your time, I don't want to die of food poisoning." He chuckled as the girl left, watching her thick hips sway.

Philippius sat on another couch and bowed awkwardly a few times. "Thank you so much for your hospitality," he said as the slave walked back in with a pitcher of wine.

"What do you think of the institution of slavery?" Socrates asked slowly as the girl poured him his drink.

The boy squirmed a bit on his couch and bit his lower lip. He didn't want another lesson today, not a rhetorical one anyway. "I'm not quite sure what I think, sir."

Socrates laughed and raised his hand. Sending the girl off with a loud slap to her ass, he winked and said, "I can't stand the thought of a human being enslaved myself, but my wife needs the help around the house. Perhaps next time I will allow her to leave her chambers and greet you. It is not good when students mix with married women, but sometimes exceptions should be made."

Philippius nodded. "Of course, of course."

There was a long awkward silence. Philippius stared at his master, who seemed content to stroke the water droplets off his own gray chest hair. Finally, the boy inhaled sharply.

"Do you really not believe in the gods?"

Socrates turned to regard Philippius. The boy looked smaller now, and his knobby knees peeked out from under his tunic like wide oranges. "Not as such, I don't think," the older man answered slowly. "If they are as capricious as the wind, they are not worth paying attention to, since we cannot control them, or depend on them, anymore than we could a storm."

"But," the boy said with a grin, "if they are the wind, wouldn't their temples be very good shelter?"

"The wind doesn't care one way or another. If the gods are real, they do not act or think like men. I do not believe in them. I am sure that men can make their own fates." The sweet scent of sausage drifted into the room.

Zeus was irate. He stalked the empty lanes of the marketplace. Thanks to his wife, he was too late for the evening rush. Most of the slaves had already bought their goods and went home. Only a few beggars and some butchers remained behind, trying to pry the last few customers of their last few obols. Beggars weren't worth considering and the butchers were only selling tripe and spoiled meat, the remnants of the day's goods. The sun was just now setting, so it was too early for the whores to begin their evening walks.

Then Zeus smelled sausage and followed his nose.

The table was covered with iron plates. Philippius had brought no less than four obols worth of sausage to his teacher, and two wineskins. A huge hunk of cheese and a half-gourd full of olives were also set out. There were three kinds of bread, one for wiping one's hands, one for eating with the meal, and the hard bread, *paximathi*, for after dinner. A large selection of sesame cakes waited on a bowl on the floor; there wasn't enough room for it on the table.

Socrates grinned at his student. "Don't eat too much. I wouldn't want you to . . . cramp up."

Philippius grinned and reached for a bunch of grapes. As he took in a deep lungful of the night air, he nearly retched. The stench of offal, shit, and vomit wafted in from a window. The two looked over and saw a beggar staring at them.

"Ho," cried the beggar, "some hospitality for a poor old man."

Socrates nodded. "Of course, old man. My slave should have left a plate out for you. We're very hospitable around here, so I always make sure she leaves provision for the poor."

The beggar shook his head, which was buried under a huge mop of matted, gray and black hair. His beard was wild and seemingly ended right under his eyelids. A cragged black hole sported a few brown teeth in the middle of his beard. His eyes were glazed over with cataracts.

"I saw no slave and no plate, kind sir," the beggar growled, seemingly annoyed.

Socrates stood up and walked to the window. "Come in then. She'll be whipped for being so forgetful. The door is three steps to your left." Behind the philosopher, Philippius shoved grape after grape into his mouth. If the stench was coming in, he needed to eat now, and a mouthful of pulp and juice would keep him from saying anything stupid for a few more seconds.

The beggar walked right in, finding his way easily enough in the dim light, and stretched out on Socrates's couch.

"Oh my," he said as he piled his sunken chest with cheese and meat. "A feast!" He tilted his head crazily, as if it was broken, and examined Philippius. "Your boy!" he called out to Socrates, "or a fuck for the night?"

Socrates silently sat on the floor, crossing his legs. "He is a student. I am his teacher." He looked at Philippius.

The boy swallowed hard and nodded. "Yes. Socrates is my master, I am sure you have heard of his wisdom."

"Can't say that I ha—" the rest of the beggar's sentence was buried in cheese and bread. He cracked the knuckles of his ten toes loudly, it sounded like a branch breaking off a tree.

Philippius piped up again, "My teacher was just telling us this morning about the ways of the gods." Socrates sighed and reached for his wine goblet, but the beggar snatched it up and emptied it in one quaff.

"Oh good good, glad to hear it," the beggar said, dyeing his beard red with the wine. He sputtered a bit more, "Even an evening fuck should be pious. The asses of the unholy are way too loose."

Socrates asked, "Where are you from, stranger?"

The beggar grabbed a handful of olives and poured them into his mouth. He chewed with his mouth open and spit out half a dozen pits, sending them bouncing across the floor. He belched and finally answered, "Oh, up there somewhere. I'm old, I forget." He waved his hands toward the north, as if dismissing the entire region.

"Thessaly?" Socrates guessed.

The beggar sat upright. "Thessaly! There are witches in Thessaly!" He leaned in close, twisting to stare at Socrates. "You calling me a witch, boy?" The old man burped again, giving the philosopher a snootful of his own dinner.

Philippius sneaked a plate of figs off the low table and placed it on his lap. He offered one to Socrates. "Teacher . . . " he began, but the old man jerked forward and knocked the fig out of the boy's hand. It bounced off the floor and landed right on the beggar's lap. He jammed the figs into his mouth, crushing them in his bony fingers. His free hand dug under the rags he was wearing to scratch his testicles.

"Must take care of your figs if you want your figs taken care of," the beggar said with a hoarse laugh. He was the only one who enjoyed the pun. Socrates again reached for the table, but the beggar planted his mud-caked feet on it first, making the plates clatter.

Socrates stood up. The beggar looked at the man. "Hey! Sit down. Tell me, what kind of religion are you teaching this boy?"

Socrates smiled to himself and nodded. Then he turned to Philippius. "Recite for your elder, boy."

Philippius opened his mouth but didn't get a syllable out when Socrates shouted, "Wrong! Today's lesson was Baucis and Philomen. How dare you forget!" The philosopher took a hold of the boy's white ear and yanked him off the couch.

"Ooowww!" the boy yelped, only to get slapped.

"Enough, boy," Socrates said, grabbing the boy's blond curls and yanking on them. Turning to the beggar he said apologetically, "He is a rockhead. I need to whip him immediately. I'm sure you understand." The beggar looked up from the plate full of sausage he had brought to his mouth.

"Whatever. Rude bastard you are, to leave a guest alone though," the beggar said. Socrates ignored that insult and pushed his young charge outside.

Philippius turned to face his teacher the moment they reached a portico. "Teacher, what did I do!" Socrates snapped a twig off a tree and leaned in to whisper to his student.

"Fake it!"

Socrates brought the switch down across the trunk of the tree. Philippius yowled, "No master, ooowww!" as if on cue.

"Have you ever seen anybody so rude?" the teacher whispered to his student as he whipped the tree again.

"You're killing me!" Philippius shouted. Then he whispered back, "Never. Nobody is that crude, that ungrateful."

Through the window they watched the beggar empty an entire wine-skin down his throat. "Nor that gluttonous," whispered Philippius.

"Exactly," the teacher whispered, hitting the trunk. Philippius didn't react so Socrates poked him with a bony elbow. "Yow!" the boy responded.

"What was your lesson for today?"

"That there are no gods?" the boy whispered. Socrates struck the tree. "Aaaah, my tender flesh! Please teacher, I'll be a good student."

"Yes, and if there are no gods, then the gods are nobody."

"And nobody is that inhospitable."

Socrates hit the tree again.

"Aiiiie! Please sire!"

"Thus, my boy . . . thus? What is your conclusion?"

"Zeus!" the boy shouted.

Luckily, the beggar didn't look up from inside. "Keep it down, boy," Socrates hissed again. "Are you aware of the myth of Baucis and Philomen?"

The boy shook his head. The old man frowned and said, "Zounds, you may get a whipping after all. They were a poor couple that Zeus turned into trees after killing everyone in their village."

"Why?" asked the boy nervously. "Did they displease him?"

"No," Socrates said with a cluck of his tongue, "they were his favorites. He wandered into a village looking for hospitality and only that old couple showed him any. Transforming men into trees is what he does to people he likes. Imagine what he might do to us!"

They both stopped and stared at the tree they were standing under.

"What do we do?"

"If there are no gods, there are no gods. We'll have to make sure there are no gods," Socrates said. Then he whispered the rest of the plan.

The pair walked back in to see the beggar wrestling with Socrates's slave. "Master," she cried and the old man let her go. Philippius's tunic was ripped and he carried a shovel. The philosopher was a bit out of breath but waved his slave away. "You may go, Terpsi."

As the slave ran off the beggar sighed and farted. "So, anything else to eat? Perhaps a nice melon?" The plates were bare. "Why that spade, boy?" he asked.

Philippius looked away and blushed, but Socrates answered. "He's dumber than a pig, thus he'll be shoveling their shit for a few days."

The beggar nodded. "Hopefully, he'll learn something about the power of the gods as well."

Philippius kneeled on the floor as his teacher took his old seat. "Actually, my masters, I do have a question about the gods."

Socrates nodded. "Go ahead, young fool." He winked at the old man. "Should be good for a laugh, eh?"

"Could Zeus create a thunderbolt terrible enough to bring down the walls of Athens?"

The beggar laughed. "Of course, child. Mortal stone masonry can't resist the will of the Sky-Father."

Socrates nodded again, agreeing. "I was a stone mason back in my day. Rock is weak, even a god's tears could wear down stone. Look at any river."

Philippius blushed. "But . . . could Zeus smite Hades with his thunderbolts?"

The beggar laughed again. "Of course, child. Zeus probably would not, since the souls of the dead would be free of their bondage. They would crawl back to the surface of the earth and outnumber the living." The beggar considered it for a moment further and then confirmed his statement. "Yes, he could do it though."

Socrates stood up and walked behind the beggar, placing his thick hands on the man's hunched shoulders. "See, boy? Elders, even the lowest of them, are full of wisdom."

"Yes, teacher."

"Of course, he is still only a beggar," Socrates said with a chuckle. "I, as a philosopher know one thing that even the Sky-Father could not do." The skies overhead darkened.

The beggar snorted as thunder rolled over the hills bordering the town. "Nonsense," he said.

Socrates grinned. "Oh, but it is true. There is no irresistible force or immovable object, after all."

The beggar rose and turned to face Socrates. "Liar. There is nothing that the gods cannot do. Mortal logic is for mortals, gods make their own way."

Socrates smiled widely. "But I am sure. I am sure there is something Zeus could not destroy, even with a thunderbolt."

Forked tongues of blue lightning arced down from the horizon. Philippius looked up nervously to glance out the window, but then lowered his eyes.

"Why are you so concerned?" Socrates asked. "What do you think it is that I have in mind?"

"Nothing, there is no such thing that a god could not do," the beggar said.

"Oh? Could Zeus destroy himself with a thunderbolt?"

Zeus raged, his disguise melting like wax. "You dare! I shall show you now what my bolts can do, even to my own personage!" The room tingled with static and ozone. Socrates felt the hair on his chest and head rise.

"No, wait!" Zeus cried. "You will not use that old trick on me." The static receded and the clouds rolled back over the ocean. He tapped his feet nervously.

Socrates glanced over Zeus's shoulder and said, "Look out behind you, my lord."

"Nor will that trick work. Look behind me indee—"

Philippius buried the blade of the spade into the skull of Zeus. The setting sun broke through the clouds as Zeus fell, dead. Black blood poured from the god's wound. For a long time, neither teacher nor student had anything to say.

Finally Socrates spoke. "Well, are you waiting for Athena to burst from the gash? Get him out of here. This is my living room."

"I supposed you'd want to kill her too, if she did show up."

"Help me get him outside. We'll throw him in the ditch after we go through his purse."

Up on high Olympus, some nymphs combed Hera's hair as she sat on her throne. She frowned as the scent of burning oxen reached her nostrils.

"Bastard, he's late to dinner again."

Socrates was later executed on charges of atheism and corrupting the youth of Athens.

Later still, much of the city died in a plague.

Old Boilers and Old Men

My boiler broke this winter, after the pedestal sink on the second floor of my home gave way and tipped over, thanks to an aging sixpenny nail. The upstairs bathroom quickly filled with water and began seeping through the gaps in the floor's tile grout. The ceiling of my kitchen, on the first floor, started leaking in spots where spackled-over drywall gave way. Once in the kitchen, the water swirled across the room and down into the basement, thanks to the holes in the floor where the water pipes stand. We quickly turned off the house feed, righted the sink and mopped up. When I turned the main valve back on, cold water hit my fifty-year-old cast iron standing pilot steam boiler which, thanks to it being February, had been running at 100+ degrees. The cheap, silvery paint-job the previous owner had applied was flaking off, and the iron chambers inside cracked when room temperature water hit red-hot iron. Isaac Newton was right when he said, after the apple landed on his head, "Physics is a bitch!"

So is getting a new boiler. Cast-iron boilers, the kind one needs when one's home is heated with those big, accordion-style radiators, are different in two crucial respects from the boilers of homes with baseboards. They cost twice as much, and are three times as heavy. I'm a child of the Internet Age. I make my living writing term papers for stupid college kids, and business obituaries for magazines nobody reads. I can't fix a boiler, and I couldn't afford a new one. So I did what anybody in my situation would do; I called on old men for help the next morning.

The first old man I called was Azad. He was the previous owner of the house, and my former landlord in Jersey City. Azad owns about nine buildings and has perfected the black art of slumlordery. When I lived in one of his other apartments, I saw garden hose in the place of piping in bathrooms, pennies jammed into fuse boxes, entire closet walls made of caulking and spackle tape, electric lights powered by inserting loose wires into outlets, and, in the backyard, a small mountain of Army surplus typewriters, stacked up against the window of my living room, exposed to the elements. He tried to sell me one when I asked about them. "Just like new, except for the leaves," he said.

I wasn't stupid enough to buy a used typewriter from this man—I own a computer, after all—but I was stupid enough to buy a house. Anyway, in the cosmic algebra of Jersey City real estate, Azad owed me.

He brought me to another old man, a man named Moe. Moe was very old, about 117, if wrinkles can be believed, and he worked in a hardware store on Duncan Avenue. Moe knows. He was on a ladder in the plumbing aisle when we approached him, and glared at us with basset hound eyes. Azad called him "Mister Moe." Mister Moe didn't acknowledge my existence, since I was obviously too young to have any worthwhile information or questions. Mister Moe must have known we were coming, since he was on a ladder doing nothing but waiting by the sealant can I needed to buy. I imagined that when my boiler went SPUNG at 2 A.M. the previous morning, Mister Moe sat up in bed across town and screamed, "A boiler! In danger!"

Moe wasn't confident the sealant would work. In fact, he said "He'll need a new boiler" to Azad. Azad shrugged. Moe was right. We poured in the sealant and turned on the water, and I had a metal box full of rain. "It's leaking too much," Azad said about twenty times. When the water drowned our ankles, he turned off the water, but too hard, breaking the switch.

We went to Home Depot. There, we were approached by a plumber named Sam. Sam instantly diagnosed our problem: we needed a new boiler, there was nothing the orange-smocked man-ape we were drawing diagrams for could do for us. He'd give us a new boiler and install it, in one day, for $1,800. He'd even, Sam The Plumber said, find us the same exact boiler, so that we wouldn't need to buy any new fittings. Finally, Sam The Plumber shook both our hands and announced, "I am Arabic!" perhaps hoping to capitalize on some secret industrial stereotype I wasn't familiar with. Italians are all in the mob, Greeks make the best greaseburgers, Jews are great with money, and when you want a bitch of a boiler installed, call upon an Arab.

Azad isn't an Arab, he's a Pakistani. As Sam walked off, he leaned in and explained, "That man isn't a real Arab. He's an Egyptian. Always watch out for an Egyptian." Another set of stereotypes only old men know. Never buy a baby from a gypsy, it'll be defective; don't stare at a Finn's shoes, you'll make him imperceptibly more self-conscious; never buy a boiler from an Egyptian, they don't really know what they're doing.

It doesn't even get cold in Egypt.

We never found the switch at Home Depot. I spent the rest of the afternoon mopping up a slow drip flood. I needed a better quality of old man. I needed to let the genie out of his bottle, no matter what the consequences. I needed to call my father.

My father is a child of the industrial age, and is entirely perplexed by my lifestyle, as his own father was by his. My father was raised on the cliffs of Ikaria in Greece, and was expected to do nothing more than strangle goats, go to church and press olives. But my father was always mechanically inclined, and mechanically inclined is an unfortunate thing to be on the poorest island in the poorest country in post-war Europe. No phones, no toilets, no internal combustion engines, no electricity, no precision instruments, no watches, no factories, no paved roads—nothing but boats, and old men didn't let strange kids near their boats. My grandfather, the blacksmith, was the most technologically advanced person in the area. His son wanted more. And eventually he got it.

Drafted into the Navy by the military junta, trained to fix diesel engines, weld steel plates while at sea and repair factory systems, my father is living in his own little space age. Physics became his bitch. TV commercials like to amaze us by explaining that the Internet can send images and information to our door at the speed of light. That isn't hard. Hard would be getting those bundles of electrons to move much slower than the speed of light. We're just along for the bitch's ride. Hard would be, hard is, getting natural gas, water, waste water, steam and exhaust to mix and trade places on demand without leaving behind a wayward drop of water, a telltale sooty smell, or without blowing up the goddamn house. Installing a boiler is hard. Installing a boiler is a bitch, said my father, paraphrasing Isaac Newton. But he could do it. There's almost nothing that can be done with two hands that he can't do.

Installing a boiler is a bitch for one simple reason: boilers are standardized. Houses are not. Boilers are designed to be moved once. Doorways are designed for people, not boilers. More often than not, the upper floors of a house don't even go up these days until the boiler is already there, in the basement.

So, my old man had to remove the old boiler, piece by piece, and I had to help. I bought a wrench and unscrewed what I could, usually having to rescrew something else back in first, or to knock off a nut with a hammer. My father noticed my wrench. Did I buy it just for this? he wanted to know. Yeah, I did. It's a piece of shit, he told me. Go get the wrench from the car. The wrench covered in grease. The wrench that smells like an oil spill. The wrench that has actually been used before.

Father: 1, Nick: 0.

I can't help but keep score when working with my father. He knows how to do everything that requires physical labor and heavy tools. He's the gawky computer nerd of the nineteenth century. He built his own home and still likes to drive by banks and point and laugh at them, because he didn't need to take a mortgage, unlike those twentieth century suckers and their credit economies. When a contractor built a home behind his backyard, my father quickly bought the lot between the two houses and poured two and a half tons of compost on the property, just to teach the guy a lesson about trying to develop in his small town. He knows everything, and he lets you know that you know nothing.

We peeled the tin off the sides of the boiler, and found cardboard and brown powder covering the works. "Don't put any in your mouth," he told me, "it's asbestos." Like I had a tablespoon standing by. While cutting away at the fittings, I banged my head against a wayward pipe hanging from the ceiling twice. My fault for not watching. My father, who is all of five foot two, banged his head against the same pipe seven times (I counted, of course). That was the pipe's fault.

Father: 1, Nick: 1.

We pulled apart the cast iron chambers of the boiler and discovered something interesting. Part of the job, the removal of the pilot light, is actually easy. Turns out my fifty year old cast-iron steam boiler with the standing pilot is actually a conversion job. It was a 110-year-old manual coal fed steam boiler, retrofitted to work with all this fancy natural gas and running water. All the old men lose a point for not recognizing this! I wanted to call Sam The Plumber, and demand he mount an expedition to raise the Titanic so he could install the exact boiler, an American Radiator Company model CL—003, right now.

Father: 0, Nick: 1.

My father speaks the language of old men, so he was incredibly useful. I ordered a new boiler and got a price quote for $2,000. He calls the same place a moment later and got a quote of $1,650. The difference was a single syllable. In response to "So, you wanna standing pilot Mclean?" I answered, "Uhm . . . yes." My father just answered "Yes."

At the store, Sanitary Plumbing Supplies, a large warehouse with every possible permutation of pipe, but without a working cash register, the old men rule. While we were there, a middle-aged man showed up, looking for a part for his toilet. What was the model of toilet? He didn't know. Did he want a rubber or plastic flapper? Dunno.

"Is your toilet," asked the suddenly very bored old man behind the counter, "one piece or two?" He didn't know. Even I know that my toilet is a two piece job. Sheesh. The middle-aged man rubbed his bald head and announced he was just going to go to Home Depot.

That man was a fool. I had already tried Home Depot, with Azad, and then again, with my father. Some eleven-year-old employee tried to sell us galvanized pipe settings, the sort very useful for putting up a fence, but only useful for boilers if you want to kill yourself and your neighbors, all at once, in a terrible explosion. There are no old men there. Home Depot is the exclusive province of the young man, of the stupid man. No wonder it's so popular.

A young man's skills do come in handy though. My father had to map out a Rube Goldbergesque pathway of black steel and copper pipe fittings. Twenty-five elbow joints, four and a half feet of 2 inch pipe. Seven two to one-and-a-half-inch reducers. Seven six-inch copper nipples. My father wasn't sure how to spell the word nipple. I was there, ready with my immense bank of knowledge, gleaned from writing five thousand crooked term papers, enough papers to buy this bitch of a house. En eye double pee el ee.

Father: 0, Nick: 2.

At the end of the day, after pulling out three quarters of a ton of cast iron and dumping it in my driveway, my father went home. I stayed home, shivering with my dog. My girlfriend and roommate spent the night elsewhere.

Father: 1, Nick: 2.

He was back the next night, Monday, after work. My father works in Brooklyn, on the docks, and reports to work at 7 A.M. That means getting up at five, squeezing into an ancient Volkswagen Jetta, and driving from lovely Port Jefferson to shithole Red Hook. He spends most of the day on the crane, four hundred feet in the air, whipped by freezing wind coming off the bay, fixing the crane. He works on those huge cranes most people only see in silhouette when crossing the Brooklyn or Manhattan bridges. Few people know that they are designed to lift sixty-ton containers from tanker ships, but that they spend most of the time lifting eighty-ton containers. Most people don't know, even the people who depend on these cranes, which includes everyone who likes . . . things, that these cranes break down a number of times a day. Most people don't know that workers have been crushed by these cranes as they roll across the piers. And only my father knows what it is like to hose the corpse meat off the huge steel wheels of one of these cranes after it runs over one of his friends. That day, everyone else was given the afternoon off, but my father, who had the most seniority—who was the oldest of the old men there—had to stay behind for two hours, with a hose and a shovel, helping the police put his pal into a garbage bag.

So after work on Monday, my Father showed up again to work on the boiler. He left at 1 A.M. and went back to the docks to sleep on a bench. He didn't want to embarrass my roommate or my girlfriend with his overnight presence. And on Tuesday, he did the same. Wednesday as well. Also Thursday. It takes a long time for one man to fit a standard boiler into a 110-year-old house.

I'm not quite sure how to score that. I get free labor, but I regret it. I want to be able to do something for my father, but there is nothing I can do that he can't, that he wants. I can make money with a computer, and this amazes him. Back when I lived at home, I'd write term papers in the living room, typing a hundred words per minute with only two fingers, and my father and his cousins and his uncles, old men even more capable than he, would just stare. I didn't have to leave the house. I didn't have to bend my back and work twice as fast because some fat foreman with mob connections wants to get home while mama's tomato sauce is still warm. I didn't have to comb my hair. Of course, neither does my father, but he feels bad about it. The only job worth having, he'd tell me as a kid, is one where you walk in with combed hair and a pressed shirt, and walk out at the end of the day the same way. Even though I've never had to hose the corpse meat off a crane, I feel bad that I'm not able to get a job like that, for him.

Father: 2, Nick: 2.

Finally it is Friday again, and my boiler works, sort of. I have to go downstairs to the basement, connect two wires together, get a little shock from the 24 volt switching mechanism, and then go back upstairs to enjoy the heat. My roommate lives down there, and whenever I go into the boiler room, he asks me, "Gonna turn the boiler on?" The old man answer would be, "Of course not. I'm just going to give her—boilers are female, like ships and other bitches—a massage. What are you, stupid?" Forty minutes later, when I go back to the basement to turn off the boiler, my roommate asks me, "Gonna turn the boiler on?" The old man answer to that stupid question would consist of a six-inch copper nipple to the head. This I know from experience. Luckily for my roommate, I'm still a young man, and we have a new boiler, one guaranteed for ten, rather than 110 years.

It's next Tuesday when my thermostat is installed. I haven't spent even five minutes with my lovely new boiler since then. I also haven't spent even five minutes with my father either, who lives in lovely Port Jefferson. He built a greenhouse last week, after work. I wrote a term paper on NAFTA, for work. He fixed a fifty-year-old tractor he bought at auction from an old bankrupt man and used it to move four tons of compost around the lot between him and his young man enemy. I wrote a little something on the thrilling topic "self-published books tend to suck" for the *Village Voice.* His own boiler broke, during what the news mistakenly called "the Storm of the Century." He fixed it himself, for free, in one day.

Father: 3, Nick: 2.

Then I realized something. Lots of immigrants' sons have these imaginary competitions with their highly skilled nineteenth-century fathers. We can never measure up, never fully be on our own, never navigate the planet without the help of an old man. Our own fathers were much smarter when they were young men. They didn't have these ridiculous hangups. They knew how to win. They left the continent their fathers were on behind them, and dove into a crazy new world without money, family or even the ability to spell the word nipple, and grew old here on their own terms. Meanwhile, I can't even consider moving further from my parents than Jersey City. After all, what if my boiler breaks again?

Final score: Father: 4, Nick: 2.

Scarlet Women Watch TV Till Dawn

Keyung Sun Park's enlightenment came to her relatively easily. She was bent over the hood of a car, her own car, pink panties down around her knees, taking it from behind when the shadows of the world began to melt away, thrust by thrust. Deep bass thudded in the club behind them and droplets of rain shook themselves free and tumbled down the windshield. Keyung could see her warped reflection. She was biting her lip, one cheek against the cold hood, tiny in the dark glass of the windshield. She could almost see me too, in my office half a town away, watching her in my mind's eye.

Keyung came, was born a new being, and saw existence for what it is the very first time. Wiping herself up with one hand, she gave the man who was just inside her a perfunctory kiss and then walked home, head up, eyes straight ahead. Later that night her date came in for his night shift job at the ward and I killed him. Rat poison in his coffee. He was too busy ever so carefully counting every stroke of his mop—anything to avoid the tedium of omniscience—to notice. He was my twelfth murder. When enlightenment is a sexually transmitted disease, one cannot be too careful.

"It's Karen," Keyung told me the next morning, when she reported for rounds. The telltale signs were all there: the short, perfunctory sentences, the sudden insistence on a pedestrian name and the inability to make eye contact with me. She had been fine with Keyung the day before, when she filled out her ID badge. Now truly enlightened, she knew that what she once thought was the real world was just a chicken wire and papier mache' imitation. It's hard for most neonates to empathize with the paper dolls who surround them. That's why I had to kill some of the others, but I knew that Keyung would find a way.

Later, I heard her talking to a pair of candy stripers about some tv show. The goofy male lead and the female lead finally kissed, even though she was far sexier than he. They had been trapped in a meat locker all night, for some reason. Keyung wasn't sure why, she hadn't been paying that much attention. She was brilliant a day ago, a moron-in-training today. Sexier now though, because she knew to drink in the joy that others experienced. Perfect. She would be able to do what I have failed to do, because my shell was just too ugly to fuck the planet. She would seduce the world for me, and drag it moaning and whimpering into a new Golden Age. I knew it, like I know everything.

#

The ward was hectic that day. Three suicidals, four kids whose parents were sick of them, two drugs and a JPC. "What's JPC?" Keyung asked me when I handed her the patient's chart. Her faux ignorance was so cute.

"Just Plain Crazy," I said. "Symptoms all over the place. Older man. Thinks he's God. Defecates on himself, claims it doesn't matter. Threatened to kill us all. We had to restrain him and give him Narcan, but he probably wasn't on anything. He's calmer now, his name is Chin. You should check in on him. Maybe you know something we don't, both of you being Chinese."

"I'm Korean. Korean-American, okay? Oh, and my parents don't own a deli," she said, rising onto the balls of her feet, a bit angry. She took a moment and inhaled, and the universe inhaled with her. I swallowed a smile, she couldn't tell about me yet.

"Just go see him. See if you can get kin information. Insurance, something!"

She turned on her heel and walked off, her razor sharp haircut bobbing just over her shoulders. Her skirt was short, and her lab coat way too long. I was barely able to stare at her calves, sleek and well-defined, wrapped in black stocking like a fleshy present. It was boiling in her. I could smell her.

Apparently, so could Chin. It took four orderlies to restrain him this time, his screaming was so loud I could barely see his mind. I jabbed a syringe full of Haldol into his thigh, and caught a glimpse of his member. Huge and purple. The lights dimmed with his consciousness, and I sent the orderlies away with a thought when Chin finally relaxed into the bed, into the straps. He was thin, too thin, and bald, with flesh pulled so taught over his skull that it looked like he was wearing a mask. Who would have screwed this poor man, and why?

I spent the afternoon arranging and rearranging next week's schedules, to make sure Keyung and I had every shift in common, and looking over the newspaper where police blotter reports and racing results nestled alongside ads for strippers with five-pointed stars for nipples and hairdos like wedding cakes. What was I looking for? A headline reading SCARLET WOMAN ATTACKS MAN AT HAND LAUNDRY, or HOMELESS PERSON LAID BY UNKNOWN ATTACKER? All there was were stories on the usual monkey-man lust for shiny things and more room to shit. *Not for much longer.* I wiped a few doughnut crumbs from the paper and got ink on my hands. *Good, now I can wash my hands instead of think,* I thought, but as I walked to the bathroom I passed Keyung on the payphone. She was leaving Glen, the man I had killed last night, a message he wouldn't be receiving.

" . . . ren, no Keyung. Just wanted to see how you were. It was pretty wild last night, but I think I have something to talk to you about. Please page me, even at work. It's sort of an emergency." I washed my hands and masturbated to orgasm three times in the stall. I gave the universe a little lick. The walls of the institution unfolded like an origami butterfly and I saw Chin's granddaughter in the grainy black and white my brain uses to conceptualize the past. Her legs were wrapped around her green-haired boyfriend, his hands all over her belly and breasts, just three nights ago. She could barely walk home that night, and chewed her fingers till they bled. Home, she sneaked into living room. Chin was asleep in the easy chair, so she sucked him off, left a note for her parents and vanished onto the streets, to spread the scarlet fire. She probably just wanted someone to talk to.

The speaker crackled overhead, "Paging Doctor Park, Paging Doctor Park," but it wasn't Glen returning Keyung's call. It was her mother, wondering where she had been last night, and if she was okay. She wasn't.

#

Keyung's legs were spread, just a little, and she touched herself with one hand while her left was on the steering wheel. She made it home though. The entire universe, which she, like myself, kept folded up in her brain, nudged the other drivers away from her and the long row of streetlights green, all the way to her apartment. That night was hard for her, but she was already learning. *Don't think, don't think, don't think about it*, I heard her think from across town. *Thank God for TVLand.* Andy Griffith saved her that night. I reached out to brush her nipples. By my will they hardened under her bra from the touch of my moist fingertip, to test her, to taste her.

She was perfumed, almost spicy. I tasted her hard, but mostly I just watched her watching tv. I watched her not thinking, watched her reading the same magazine article over and over again; not "The Girl's Guide To Great Orgasms" but "Buy A Like-New Used Car, Online!" because those were the only 1000 words in *Cosmo* with no sex in them. I pinched, and nibbled and tugged at her in all sorts of places, inside and out, but she watched television till dawn, and I watched her. In a small, sane little corner of her brain though, she knew, and she was watching me, watching her.

Finally, when she slept, bathed in the blue glow of an infomercial, I made my bed. I measured the angle of my covers and the distance between the hem of my sheets and the floor at six-inch intervals around all four sides then fixed the sheets. With my thoughts nothing but a gray buzz of boredom, I got into bed and slept a dreamless sleep. Necessary, you know. When the consciousness is omniscient, the subconscious is insane. I woke up erect, as usual and thought of Keyung while I masturbated.

That morning I saw her over the rim of my cup of chocolate pudding, the near flavorless institutional pudding we feed the patients, giggling again with two new friends. She was the only resident who spent time with the orderlies, the stripers, the physical plant workers. The puddin'heads. *Karen*, they called her. *Karen, do you want to go to the movies? Karen, do you like my shoes? Karen, you look pretty today, I love your nails. You're not like the other doctors, Karen; you're so nice. We can talk to you, like a real person. Did you see this show? Don't you like this food? What about that celebrity, isn't she a whore?*

And yet, Keyung Sun Park still stood erect amidst her little tribe of troglodytes. She was alive, still regal even when mindlessly flapping her lips like a goldfish in a bowl, ready to be my priestess whore. She was about to say something back to them, to push beyond the mortal and show the sacks of chemical reactions and hastily-stored calories around her a thing or two about the universe. If they didn't understand her, and they wouldn't understand her, she'd find herself on her knees, blowing and sucking on the lot of them just to get them to *listen.*

Then I felt the circuit breaker in her brain click solidly. "Thanks," she said, bright as a penny. "Too many of these residents and doctors think they're God or something. But I like to hang out with real people. Oh, have any of you guys seen Glen at all today? He's been out sick or something, but hasn't called." She snapped her gum like it was punctuation. Nobody knew, so the notion of Glen evaporated. She was still afraid to look for him with her mind. For a moment I thought she might be too cowardly to carry out my plans for her. I thought of my pistol, then pushed it out of my mind before it could materialize in my hand.

Keyung changed the subject herself, "Anyone going to see Green Day next month?" The skirt she wore had a slit halfway up the thigh, and she went braless. I could feel the fabric of her sweater against her chest, against my chest. Later, in the tv room, she was watching *Oprah* when I told her that I needed her to pull a double shift that night. With me.

The night shift was insane, more insane than usual. Somewhere out there, Chin's granddaughter was screwing everything with legs. Half-crazed teen boys, still bubbling with hormones like cooking sausages, older men with piss-stained sweatpants and featureless gray jackets, girls with collars of purple bruises around their necks. We had to move some of them upstairs, or to other hospitals, to keep them away from one another.

There were a dozen of them, and they were hungry for it all, their minds wide open and waiting for the terrible world to jump right in. The only thing that could keep them from the pain of every hungry child, the terror of every late-night burst of gunfire, the shutter of every death rattle was to slam their fists against their own groins, or to devolve into the miasma of the television and the pop song. I hid for twenty minutes to jerk off in the janitor's closet, because Keyung had been hovering by the bathrooms all night, always five minutes from a mumbled excuse and a crotch slamming session of her own. In his bed, Chin screamed through the Thorazine haze and ejaculated till he was dry.

After lights out, Keyung came into my office. I was watching a home shopping channel on the little black and white tv I kept on my desk.

"Ms. Park," I said.

"Doctor Winston, I . . . " she stopped, her mouth open, her lips red and hungry. The shadow of her tongue flicked across her too-white teeth. I concentrated on the television. One hundred twenty-eight cubic zirconium rings to go. Make that one hundred twenty-six. "Bad night tonight."

"Mmm," I said, blandly. "Your psychiatric round is almost over. Nobody really likes it. But . . . "

"You're not . . . supposed to like it, you're supposed to do it," she finished with me. "I know. I'm dreading ICU. A death or two, every single shift. God, how can anyone stand it?" She sniffed, almost teared up, and tugged at the hem of her skirt.

"I've been meaning to discuss appropriate wardrobe with you. You've been wearing unacceptable clothing all week."

"Where's Glen?" Keyung demanded, her tiny hands slapping the edge of my desk, fingers wrapping around the corner. Her knuckles shifted color from the lightest of yellows to white. I couldn't keep my eyes from her cleavage. "What did you . . . do?" she asked.

Very dramatic. I was tempted to answer *How did you . . . know* to taunt her, but instead I sighed and glanced back at the television. "The contagion has to be contained. Not everyone can handle it. Not like . . . "

" . . . you."

"If by you, you mean me, yes," I said. "If by you, you mean you, well then, we'll have to see. It depends on what you decide to do with your new gift. Of course, you can *know* what to do. You can know whatever you like. Most people seem ill-suited for the tasks of spreading enlightenment though."

"Summer camp, up by Syracuse," she started, standing erect again. My groin tingled. "What were you, ten years old, maybe? It was one of those hippie-dippie camps, no flag football, no bonfires, just sing-alongs and arts and crafts. One of the counselors was named Bandana Bob. Lennon glasses, long beards, liked to give blowjobs to the boys in their beds, after singing most of them to sleep with his guitar and a few rounds of 'Johnny Row Your Boat Ashore'. He didn't even know his chakras were inflamed, and that he was spreading enlightenment with every suck."

She was confident, but I only smiled at the tv.

"And how many people have you had since then? Bath houses? Dorm rooms? Glory holes? There was Jerry and Kimberly and Brad and . . . " and her eyes glazed over. She was swimming in a thousand memories, a thousand pairs of scuffed knees and elbows, and a thousand licks and taunting nibbles. And after, an even dozen bloody deaths, because my partners just weren't good enough. Well, most of them weren't. Keyung plucked that stray thought from my mind, an errant eyelash from a lover.

Her expression melted. "You killed Glen. No. Wait, you paid Glen to suck your dick, just to give him . . . the contagion. Because you knew he wanted me, and would use his power to make me take a fucking. Then you killed him," she said, practically shouting the word *killed*, but then she calmed. " Because he was greedy, insane from the wisdom. Out for his own self-interest . . . "

I pointed to a small banner I kept between the diplomas on my wall. It was red, festive, marked with golden pictographs. "Ms. Park, ever hear the saying, 'Before enlightenment, chop wood, carry water. After enlightenment, chop wood, carry water'? Even the wisest sages have to know what is important. Glen wasn't important. You are." I pointed to my left temple, "In here is what you need to do. My plan. My utterly perfect plan to save the world from famine, from nuclear war, from having both its past and its future wiped out by stupdity. I'm not going to tell you the plan. You're strong. You're smart. The world, literally, is at your feet. You'll figure out what it is that needs to be done. You wanted to help people before. You want to help them now. Just be careful who you sleep with. Find men and women who can handle wisdom, and who need it. Otherwise . . . it's sad having to strangle a dream. It's hard to kill when you feel all the pain in the world."

I turned back to the tv and fed Keyung a bit of racial memory. An afternoon in Dachau. Everyone's afternoon—scraggly prisoners and sharp-dressed smiling Nazi soldiers alike. Keyung fell to the floor, twitching. When she stopped, I stepped over her, said "Pardon me, Karen. I have to go kill someone else now," and crossed the common area, to Chin's room, and smothered him with his pillow. Thirteen. I had to do it; the hospital couldn't hold him past 72 hours.

Through the wall I heard some familiar babbling. Good and evil, all decided. How to end hunger, expressed as a haiku. The actual ratio of chance and individual action that led us poor people around like dogs on a leash. I left a packet of razorblades where the two young boys who were sharing the room next to Chin's would find it before the morning. *Fate or free will?* I dared think to myself, but then pushed my little death wish for those poor kids aside to concentrate on a jingle I heard on the radio this morning.

Keyung woke eventually, and wandered outside into the parking lot, tripping on her own high heels. She took them off to run to the curb, dirty water oozing through the fabric of her panty hose and squishing between her beautiful, painted toes. If not for the cold and grit in the water, I would have taken them in my mouth from across the ether, and sucked on each one.

It didn't take her long to hail a ride. When she raised her hand, every cabbie in the city slowed down instinctively, just for a moment. One stopped in front of Keyung and she dove in.

"Drive. West side. The rest area. I'll be worth your while," she said through pursed lips. She squeezed her legs together to feel the warmth of her crotch. In a moment, they were parked. I could feel the hole in the vinyl upholstery, left by a cigarette burn, scratch the flesh of her ass.

I could feel her fingers in the man's hair, in my hair, tightening around our scalps like ropes. Her thighs were heavy on the man's lap, his penis all but lost inside her. He kept the meter running. 5.20. 5.50. 5.80.

"Listen to me. You know it now," she said. "You can feel it, can't you, Smapdi Kayani? You're not just a piece of shit little immigrant working at 3AM for an extra twenty bucks now, you're a fucking god-king, and you just fucked your queen." The cabbie's eyes were wide, with fear, with love, with knowing. He licked his lips, and ignored the teeth of his fly biting into his flaccid penis.

"Yes, yes, I know. Why? Why?" he asked, his voice so desperate, almost a song.

"I don't know either. I haven't been able to think about it. I haven't been able to do anything but distract myself with jerking off and *Star Trek* reruns. You're going to tell me, you understand, and then you're going to go nuts and drive into the closest river. Keep your windows open. Wear your seatbelt. Floaties are no fair." She growled and bit him hard on the lip. He was stock still, but I felt it, I felt it across town, and my mouth bled too.

Phantom lines of pain danced across my wrists. The boys at the ward, I felt their deaths and was distracted, just for a second. A second was all it took though. Then twin headlights blinded my mind's eye and the newest sexual sage, Smapdi, drove right into the loading dock at the back of my mind.

"In the olden times," he told Keyung, "there were temple whores. You prayed, you paid, you made love on a bench or a special room. You caught a glimpse of heaven, being inside those women, smelling their skin, kissing their breasts. The wealthiest got the most beautiful, the virginal. Scarlet women they were called after that, because the blood, the blood was life. The blood on the sheets enlightened. The priest-kings knew how to rule . . . "

"And now," Keyung said, "Now, every damn janitor and cabbie is enlightened, is that it? The scum of the earth, sucking and screwing at suburban wife-swapping parties, in phone booths, and in parking lots. Any fifteen-year-old without too much acne can get a kiss from God. But nobody is really giving the tired old men in suits, the ones who run the planet, the fucking they deserve . . . "

"And who in America could make love with me? Brown, poor, immigrant?" Smapdi said, hollow with the realization. Keyung wouldn't have to give a mental command to make sure he drove into the river, he was going to of his own free will. Fate was my plaything for Keyung. She was smart enough, beautiful enough, and now both enlightened and insane enough to lead the world into a new Golden Age, one hurried blowjob or broom closet assignation at a time.

"What a waste," she said, to herself. She slid off her victim and out into the night. Smapdi drove into the river.

#

There was a 6AM Amtrak train to Washington D.C. Keyung was on it, and reading the schedule over and over again, memorizing the times so she wouldn't have to hear the swirling brains of three hundred other commuters. She wore slacks that day, with a tight black sweater and too much eye makeup, to look not beautiful, but accessible. Her lipstick was red and thick, thick enough to leave a half-kiss stain on the rim of a glass in a Beltway bar.

It took me most of the afternoon to track down Chin's granddaughter. I had to take an extended lunch to find the little whore. She had balled some of her school chums; I found three of them on a park bench by the handball courts. One of them, a young boy in a black coat, was animated. His hair, long bangs swooped down over his eyes, but the sides closely shaved, danced in front of him as he discussed the existence of God and what He meant, exactly, by the thirteen million corpses piled up during the Holocaust. It was a comma, he said, of a very complex sentence. The girl was in a daze, reeking of ganja, and the third, another girl, sat with her eyes closed and headphones blasting some saccharine pop substitute for love.

I raised a curtain of ignorance about my person and shot them all. Fourteen, fifteen, sixteen. How many more of these insane little bastards to go, I didn't want to know. But I could have known, in an instant.

That night, Keyung found her first, right outside D.C, in Virginia. It was a Holiday Inn bar, and he was there for the band, believe it or not. The drummer was a friend of his, and had mentioned that sometimes you can get action in a Holiday Inn bar. Lonely women sometimes want revenge on their husbands for their infidelity, and payback is always a bitch. *A bitch, get it?*

Jim was his name, and he was thin, with a large head perched atop a pencil-neck. He had a large nose and beady black eyes—he looked for all the world like a plucked turkey in a cheap suit. Keyung smiled at him and asked the time. He smiled back and gave it to her, and he gave it to her exactly. It wasn't almost eight-thirty, it was *exactly eight twenty-seven, pee em*, he told her.

What did he do, she asked. He worked for the Department Of Labor. Workplace safety issues. He'd been on the job for years. He liked helping people. Papa had been an autoworker till his elbows ground to powder on the assembly line. He hummed along to "Sentimental Journey" with the band while Keyung drank her Singapore Sling and thought. She knew he wouldn't be able to handle her gift, not for more than a week or so before he nailed his own tongue to his jaw to keep from speaking. That might be long enough though. She knew Jim wasn't the type to have friends, but he was the type to want to get off. He worked with people, people he already fantasized about. They might have friends. They might even go to fund-raising parties, or meet a Congressperson on some handshake tour deal. And, after all, she had to start somewhere, didn't she? Someone had to fuck the world back into shape, so a billion black babies didn't howl from hunger in her dreams.

Jim wasn't even that bad looking; if he were fifteen years younger and in black, he could have been in a band himself, doing groupies in parking lots. Besides, she was going to be here for a long time, having drinks, meeting men and women, and enlightening them, the better classes of people. It would be years before her looks failed her, and she could wait. *The world is worth it*, she thought, and I smiled. She would drag this world screaming into enlightenment, one climax at a time. Then I'd finally be able to rest. Jim looked over Keyung and smiled too, for different reasons. He could hardly wait. I could hardly wait. Keyung gave George the once over, from bushy eyebrows to paunch, and shuddered.

It was going to be a long sleepless night, for all of us.

Travel Between Heavenly Bodies

The first rule of the routine space mission is that there is no such thing as a routine space mission. We were to drop off The Commodore on Altair VI, but he, resplendent in red velour and tight black slacks, went mad mere moments into our trek and threw himself at the helm's control panel, his chest slamming against the Physics-Breaking Button. The lights dimmed, gravity shifted from left to right forcing us all to jerk and sway helplessly, and the turbines of the ship, my one true love, screamed as we hurtled past papier mache' planets and Christmas light stars. We found ourselves stranded many light-years away, the magic rocks within our engine wawmb wawmb wawmmmbing pitifully. The Chief Alcoholic didn't like that, not at all.

As I recorded in my diary, we found ourselves orbiting a strange planet. The Commodore had to be sedated by the Man Who Is Almost Always Wrong, but even with enough dope to knock out an Antarean Bull Moose in his veins he cried out, shrieking like a Charlie Parker saxophone solo. He needed to be on the surface, and now! So did we. There were more magic rocks below. We'd have to negotiate with the natives, cure the Commodore, repair our precious ship and press the Physics-Breaking Button, hold it down even, till we found ourselves back on course.

I selected an away team from among the only eight people I'd ever met from among my crew of hundreds. The Man Who Is Almost Always Wrong had to come, of course, so he could investigate the planet for whatever strange energies made The Commodore go so insane. To balance him out, I brought along The Man Who Is Always Right: they so loved to bicker. And some Anonymous Nobody to carry our Useless Weapons. I chose myself to lead the team, of course.

On the surface, we waved around tape recorders that beeped and booped incoherently. The terrain was hardscrabble chicken wire draped in fabric, the sky was painted a dull pinkish-gray. We were so enraptured by our powerful noisemakers that we never even saw Nobody wander off, not till he howled and died. We found his corpse green and sizzling, and standing over the body the most beautiful woman on this world or any other. She wore a mighty bouffant hairdo whose height rivaled the geysers of Coridan IV, a tinfoil tunic, and silvery go-go boots. The Man Who Is Almost Always Wrong frowned at me while I swaggered up to her and told her my job and middle initial. She said her name was Klaxora and when she spoke it was as though she shifted into a soft focus.

In the distance somebody strummed a space harp. Poorly.

Klaxora needed our help. She had used advanced cardboard boxes and copyright-free sound effects to gain the power of mental telepathy. Promising strange star love, she had mentally reached out for The Commodore, for only so brave and white a man as he could save her from the ravages of the loin-clothed barbarians of the northern continent of her world. The Man Who Is Always Right looked dubious. He signaled me with his eyebrow.

"You. Killed. My. Man," I said, slowly, so the universal translator could keep up. "How. Could. You. *Do!* Such. A . . . thing?" When I looked into her deep blue eyes I knew that I'd believe her answer, no matter how ridiculous it was. His hair had dipped below his earlobes and even touched the edge of his collar, Klaxora said. She thought he was a barbarian trying to trick her. Then she flung herself into my arms and wept. I cradled her, the way a man with strong space-faring arms should.

Once, Klaxora told us, as we stood around in a day-glo cave, her people, also called the Klaxora, and the barbarians lived as one society. But under the influence of a sinister siren call, most of the citizens of a once-mighty civilization cast off their crinkly chrome garments and turned their backs on a life of science to live in the woods like filthy animals. Their mental faculties had degraded so that even her telepathy machines were no use against them. Barbarians responded only to the psychedelic jungle rhythms that had lured them into the countryside. She was the only one left, and she needed a man, one who would help her repopulate the planet, reclaim the scientific achievements of her ancestors, as represented by a single blinking red light, and bring harmony out of chaos.

Oh, how I wanted to be that man. The way Klaxora's bosom felt against my muscled chest, the crinkle of foil against slick velour, the promise of endless procreative sex rather than the dreary diplomatic humping that was my duty as a Space Corps captain. I turned to the Man Who Is Almost Always Wrong. "It's love, Jim," he said, "but not as we know it." The Man Who Is Always Right reminded us that what we really needed were magic rocks to power our Physics-Breaking Buttons, so that we could continue our endless mission.

The offer was a simple one—she'd give us rocks to get off the planet, and in exchange, I'd get my rocks off with her. For all eternity, kept alive by celluloid and syndication rights. But then, with a horrible splat of acid jazz and tribal drums, the barbarians appeared! The Man Who Is Almost Always Wrong fell easily, but Right and I fought like lions. I raised my arms high, clenched my hands together, and pummeled barbarian after barbarian. The Man Who Is Always Right disabled his foe with a pinch to the shoulder. But still they came at us, one at a time!

. . . far overhead, the Chief Alcoholic sat in my chair fretting over the ship's decaying orbit, but he could not contact us, no matter how many times he played the recording of two notes on a pennywhistle. "Wheee-oop! Whee-oop!" The communications chief heard nothing in her earring either. She never did. But her miniskirt, aaah . . .

I spun wildly on my heel, looking for another enemy to fight, but all that remained were the still bodies of our battered foes. And Klaxora was gone!

We tracked her and her kidnappers to an outcropping that looked exactly like the field we had entered on, stage left, mere minutes before. The barbarians had bound her to a stake right in the middle of the outcropping. She twisted against poorly tied knots and cried out plaintively for her captain! O Captain! And then the song began.

It sounded so strange . . . and yet, so familiar! Thump, thump thumpthump. Thumpthump. Thuuump. Thummp. Thummmp. The barbarians swayed and muttered. "In. A. Gadda. Da. Vida . . . " One of the fiends raised a rubber machete to Klaxora's milky-white neck. The Man Who Is Almost Always Wrong tried to hold me back, but I pushed him away and rushed to the center of the moot.

"No! You cannot! Do this!" I shouted, ready to fight but all the more eager for peace. "That song! Where did you get that song?"

His face well tanned, the head barbarian lowered his machete. "This is the song. Of our people," he explained, words hard and rare in his mouth.

"No! Not your people! It is an old earth song, from . . . " I turned to The Man Who Is Always Right. "I believe Terrans refer to that era as 'the sixties,' according to the old calendar based on your ancient myths of a long-haired savior," he explained.

"Long . . . hair?" the barbarian asked, and he shook his own blond mane to show his approval. My naked neck beaded with perspiration—ah, for the sideburns of my Academy days.

"Yes! Long hair! The sixties! Free love! The hippy movement! That song! The one you are singing! An ancient Earth ditty!" I took a deep breath and tried to remember the lyrics. "In. The. Garden. Of. Eee-den, bay-bee. Don't you know I—yes, I!" I said, thumping my chest, "that I love you!"

. . . in the inky blackness of space, the two barely visible lengths of fishing line holding my precious ship in orbit began to sag and jiggle . . .

"Stop the hate! You must love, like your sacred song says!" I cried out, taking only the briefest of moments to glance at my Klaxora. She began to smile, as did the longhaired barbarians. "Yes," their chief intoned solemnly. "Yes," his tribe of six repeated.

"Yes," said Klaxora, who began to fade from view. All of them began to dissolve as a disembodied chorus struck an operatic note. Above the place the people of Klaxora once stood floated an Omnipotent Blob Of

Light, glowing and crackling like burnt film emulsion in the 35-millimeter sky.

"Hello Captain," it said in a legion of harmonious voices. "We are Klaxora."

"Fascinating," muttered The Man Who Is Always Right and Always Right Behind Me.

"What is it, Jim!" demanded The Man Who Is Almost Always Wrong.

"We are Klaxora," the Klaxora repeated. She/they/it spilled light on us like we were standing at a soundstage as she/they/it spoke. "Millennia ago, our telepathic gifts, augmented by technology, allowed us to leave behind our bodies and become beings of pure thought . . . "

" . . . pure energy," said The Man Who Is Always Right, pretending to read a dial from the top of his tape recorder.

"Before our last daughter joined us in eternal bliss and contemplation, she chose to wait out the lonely centuries, until a man could teach her the true meaning of love. Bored during her long vigil, we created a race of enemies to test her courage. The Klaxora you knew was never ever in any danger."

"What is this! You can't just toy with human lives in this way! Right now, up in sick bay, a Space Corps Commodore is probably chewing through his leather restraints, ready to throw himself out of an airlock just to *meet* Klaxora," said The Man Who Is Almost Always Wrong.

"You are wrong," the Omnipotent Blob Of Light explained. "We have cured him of the negative effects of Klaxora's telepathic rays. We have also temporarily righted your ship's orbit. Everything is now precisely as it was forty-eight minutes ago. You may also claim the entire planet and its resources. We have evolved far beyond the needs of propulsion, and indeed, perhaps one day you hew-mans might do the same."

The lights dimmed. Klaxora was gone.

Needless to say we contacted our superiors and they made plans to mine the planet hollow. The Chief Alcoholic used a soundboard's volume lever to bring us back to the ship. "Vvrrrrreeeeeeee!" it sang. "Vvrrrrreeeeee!"

"That's the second rule of routine missions," I said into the primitive Earth microphone right over my head. I was safe, on my bridge, and with my faithful crew. I never had the same shyness or reticence of many other starship captains. I recorded my log right in front of everybody, whether they cared to listen or not. "There is no greater love a captain has than for his ship." I frowned, thinking of that beautiful girl. "I'll miss Klaxora though, wherever she is, out among the stars."

"Yep," said The Man Who Is Almost Always Wrong. "She had a heavenly body, Jim. But now she is a heavenly body."

"This time, Doctor, you are correct," said The Man Who Is Always Right.

And then we laughed and laughed, the whole crew. Except for the Man Who Is Always Right. O, how we laughed!

Then I ordered the Physics-Breaking Button pressed and we were off on another adventure.

Publication History

"The Daniel Boone Of Jersey City," *Mr. Beller's Neighborhood*, 2001.
"Your Life, Fifteen Minutes From Now," *Talebones*, 2000.
"Brother Theodore Is Dead," Disinfo.com, 2001.
"Time Of Day," *Strange Horizons*, 2002.
"Do The Wall Street Hustle," *Gadfly Online*, 2002.
"The Armory Show," *Razor*, 2002.
"It's An Honor To Be Nominated," *Mr. Beller's Neighborhood*, 2002.
"Impression Sunrise," *Speculon*, 2002.
"Why I Flame," *Village Voice*, 2000.
"Joey Ramone Saves The World," *Razor*, 2003.
"The Dead Don't Stay Dead," *Wide Angle NY*, 2003.
"Beer On Sunday," *Horrorfind*, 2002.
"How To Rid The World Of Good," *Everything You Know Is Wrong* (Disinformation Books), 2002.
"The Birth Of Western Civilization," *The Whirligig*, 2002.
"Old Boilers And Old Men," *Mr. Beller's Neighborhood*, 2001.
"Scarlet Women Watch TV Till Dawn," *Suicide Girls*, 2003.
"Travel Between Heavenly Bodies," original to this volume.

Printed in the United States
16826LVS00001B/369